Projects in
GENERAL
METALWORK

Projects in GENERAL METALWORK

M. J. RULEY
*Director, Industrial Arts
and
Vocational Education
Tulsa, Oklahoma*

McKnight & McKnight Publishing Company
Bloomington, Illinois

Revised Edition

Copyright 1968

by McKnight & McKnight Publishing Company

All rights reserved. No part of this book may be reproduced, in any form, without permission in writing from the publishers.

Lithographed in U.S.A.

First Edition Copyright 1951

Preface

The projects in this book are offered with the hope that you will enjoy making them and that when completed you will find satisfaction in their use.

The articles suggested are easy to make, require only the ordinary shop equipment, and use very little material. Accompanying each project is a list of materials needed, suggested references to give you the necessary instruction, and the proper sequence of operations to follow in completing the object.

It is the sincere hope that those who use this series of projects will find several of them helpful and stimulating, and that they may experience the satisfaction of achievement in a piece of work well done. As your skill and ability develop, you may wish to design and construct more difficult pieces.

Acknowledgment is hereby given to Mr. S. S. Orman of Tulsa Central High School for preparing the drawings, and to instructors in general metals, Tulsa public schools, for valuable help in reading and checking, and to others for assistance in preparing the manuscript and offering valuable suggestions.

M. J. RULEY

Contents

Project 1 - - Bottle Openers - - - 10
Project 2 - - Utility Bracket - - - 12
Project 3 - - Small Hammer - - - 14
Project 4 - - Turner - - - 16
Project 5 - - Towel Rack - - - 18
Project 6 - - Charcoal Tongs - - - 20
Project 7 - - Hose Holder - - - 22
Project 8 - - Garden Trowel - - - 24
Project 9 - - Jar Opener - - - 26
Project 10 - - Candelabra - - - 28
Project 11 - - Scoop - - - 30
Project 12 - - Tool Tray - - - 32
Project 13 - - Spice Rack - - - 34
Project 14 - - Tooth Brush Holder - - - 36
Project 15 - - Dust Pan - - - 38
Project 16 - - Memo Pad Holder - - - 40
Project 17 - - Picture Frame - - - 42
Project 18 - - Weeder - - - 44
Project 19 - - Toasting Fork - - - 46
Project 20 - - Door Knocker - - - 48
Project 21 - - Flower Bud Holder - - - 50
Project 22 - - Flower Pot Holder - - - 52
Project 23 - - Pin-Up Lamp - - - 54
Project 24 - - Pin-Up Lamp - - - 56
Project 25 - - House Marker - - - 58
Project 26 - - Window Sill Pot Holder - - - 60
Project 27 - - Bicycle Luggage Carrier - - - 62
Project 28 - - Lawn Glass Holder - - - 64
Project 29 - - Door Grill - - - 66
Project 30 - - Garden Hose Holder - - - 68
Project 31 - - Coping Saw Frame - - - 70
Project 32 - - Soldering Copper - - - 72
Project 33 - - C-Clamp - - - 74
Project 34 - - Marking Gauge - - - 76
Project 35 - - Screwdriver - - - 78
Reference List - - - 80

Project 1—Bottle Openers

Either of these openers is easy to make. Lengthen the handle of B and add side pieces of fine wood to make a deluxe opener.

Material Required:
Opener A
    1 piece band iron, 1/8 x 1¾ x 3¾

Opener B
    1 piece band iron, 1/8 x ¾ x 4¾

References:
Ludwig, *Metalwork Technology and Practice*
Dragoo & Reed, *General Shop Metalwork*
Smith, *Units in Bench Metalwork*

Procedure:

Opener A
1. Get out material.
2. Lay out design.
3. Transfer design to metal.
4. Cut out inside by drilling, chiseling and filing.
5. Shape outside with saw and file.
6. Drill 3/16" hole in handle.
7. File edges smooth.
8. Draw file flat surfaces.
9. Polish with emery cloth.
10. Check.

Opener B
1. Get out material.
2. Cut to length.
3. Lay out.
4. Center punch for holes.
5. Drill holes as shown.
6. Cut slot and shape as shown.
7. File ends half-round.
8. File edges smooth.
9. Draw file flat surfaces.
10. Polish with emery cloth.
11. Check.

Related Study:
Laying out
Using a hack saw
Using a file
Drilling
Draw filing
Emery cloth

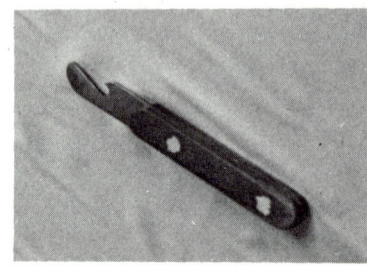

PAGE 10

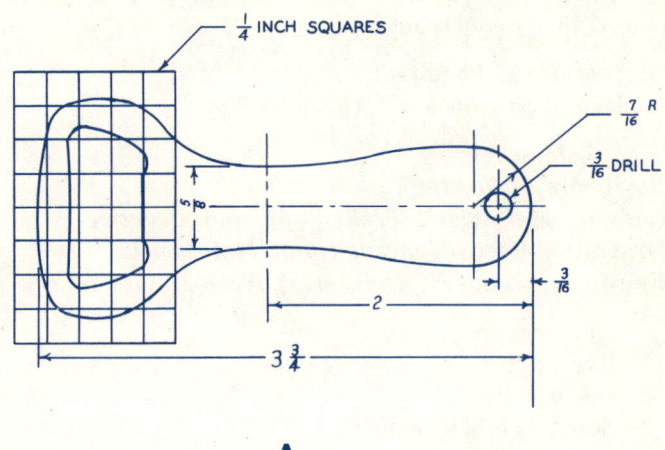

A

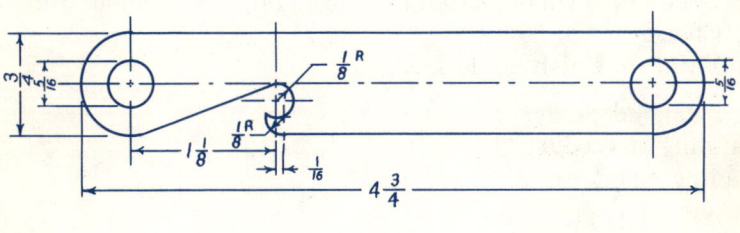

B

BOTTLE OPENERS

Project 2—Utility Bracket

This is a simple bench metal project that may be used around the home. A number of fundamental tool processes are experienced in its construction.

Material Required:
1 piece band iron $\frac{1}{8}$ x $\frac{1}{2}$ (or $\frac{3}{4}$) x $7\frac{3}{8}$

References:
Boyd, *Metalworking*
Ludwig, *Metalwork Technology and Practice*
Dragoo & Reed, *General Shop Metalwork*
Feirer & Lindbeck, *Industrial Arts Metalwork*

Procedure:
1. Read print.
2. Get out stock.
3. Square ends to length.
4. Layout with rule, dividers, and scriber.
5. Center punch for holes.
6. Drill $\frac{3}{16}''$ holes.
7. Saw off corners and file to lines.
8. Finish with emery cloth.
9. Bend as shown on dotted lines of print. Use hammer and vise.
10. Check.
11. Paint or finish as desired.

Related Study:
Planning procedure
Reading prints
Measuring
Laying out
Drilling
Filing
Bending
Sawing

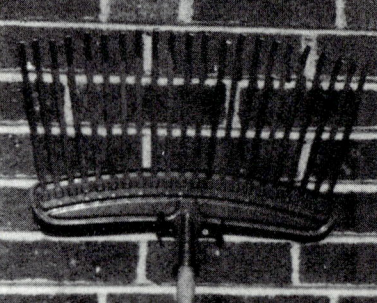

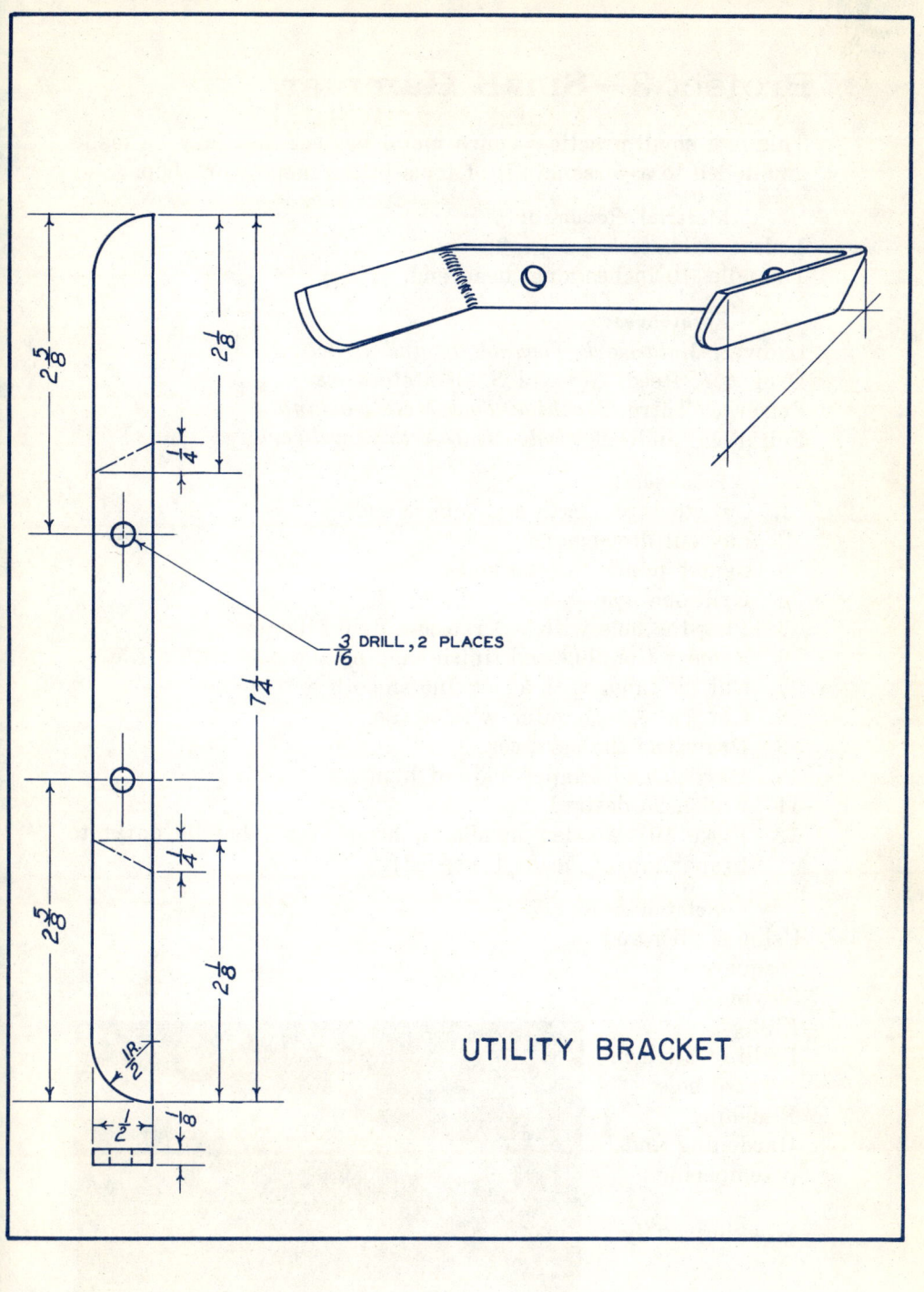

UTILITY BRACKET

Project 3—Small Hammer

This is a small practical bench metal project that may be made and added to a personal kit of tools in the home workshop.

Material Required:
1 piece mild steel, $\frac{1}{2}$ x $\frac{1}{2}$ x $3\frac{5}{8}$
1 handle, 10 inches long, head end, $\frac{5}{16}$ x $\frac{1}{2}$

References:
Ludwig, *Metalwork Technology and Practice*
Dragoo & Reed, *General Shop Metalwork*
Feirer & Tatro, *Machine Tool Metalworking*
Feirer & Lindbeck, *Industrial Arts Metalwork*

Procedure:
1. Cut stock to length and square ends.
2. Lay out dimensions.
3. Center punch for the holes.
4. Drill one hole $\frac{5}{16}''$.
5. Plug the hole with $\frac{5}{16}''$ rod and drill other hole.
6. Remove the plug and finish shaping the hole with a file.
7. Cut the taper with a saw and smooth with a file.
8. Cut the $\frac{1}{16}''$ chamfer with a file.
9. Draw file the surfaces.
10. Harden and temper ends of hammer.
11. Finish as desired.
12. Place 10" wooden handle in head (work handle down to proportion of head if needed).

Related Study:
Using scriber and square
Sawing
Filing
Drilling an elongated hole
Finishing
Hardening and tempering
Steel
Working safely

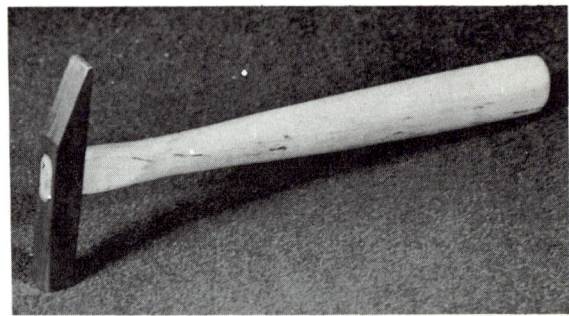

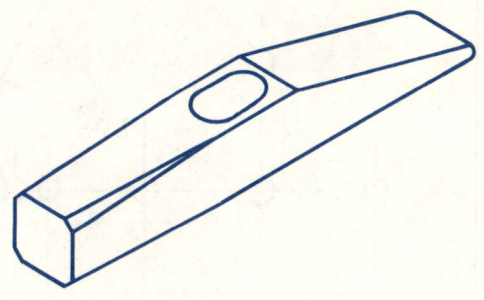

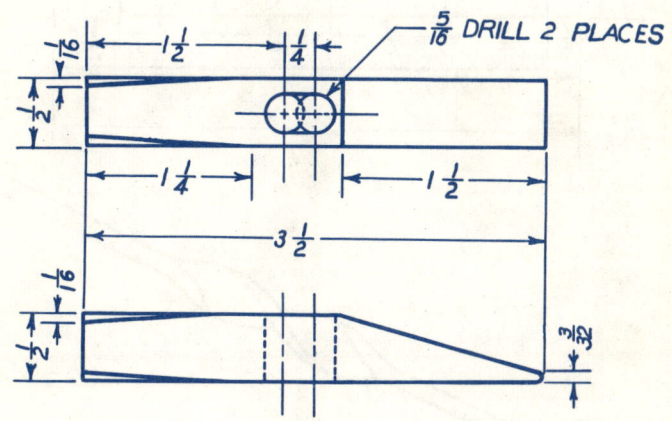

HAMMER

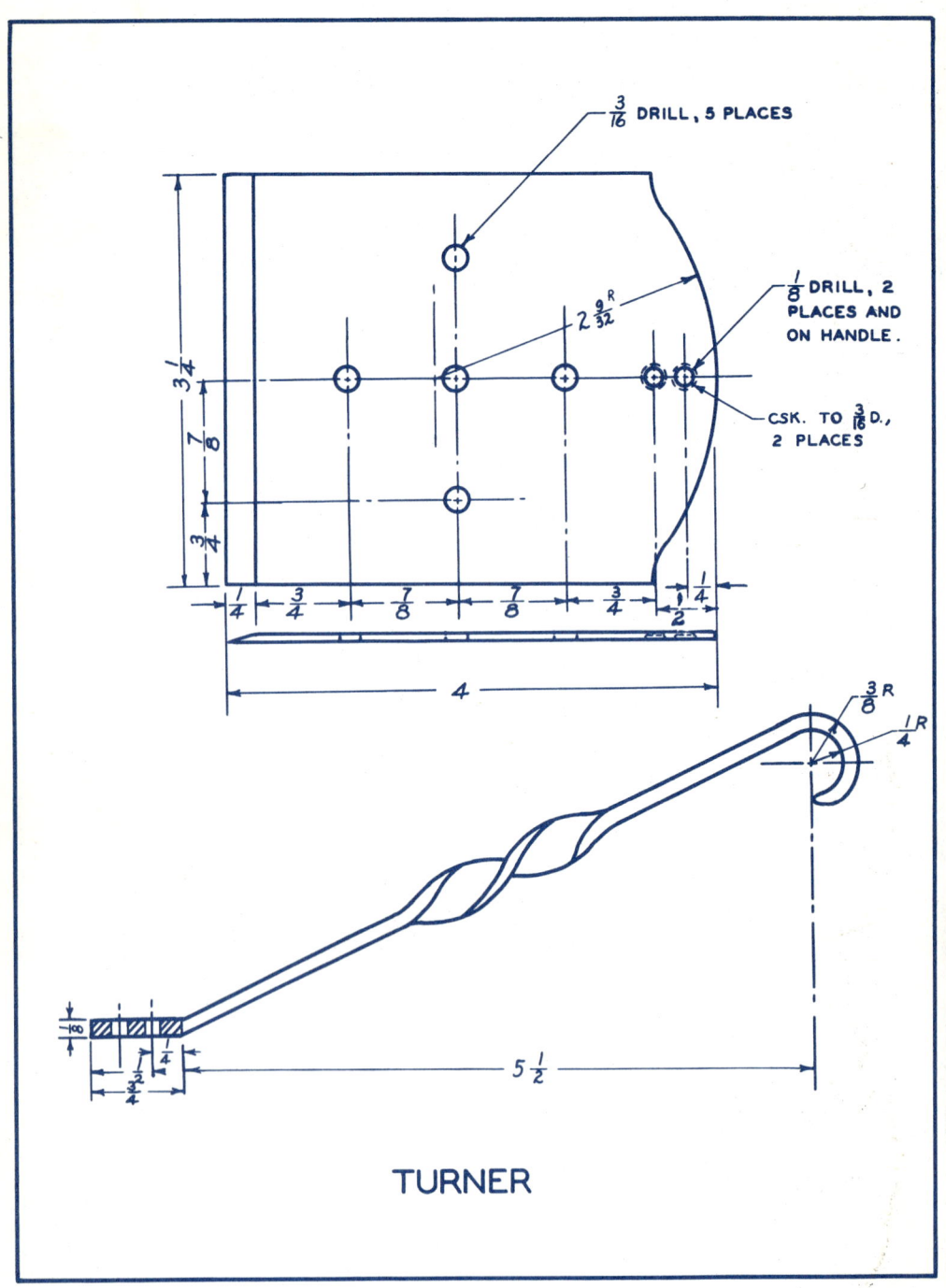

Project 4—Turner

A turner that may be carried on a camping trip, used at the barbecue pit, or in the kitchen.

Material Required:
1 piece band iron, $\frac{1}{8}$ x $\frac{1}{2}$ x 11
1 piece #18 gauge black iron, $3\frac{1}{4}$ x 4
2 rivets, soft iron, round heads, $\frac{1}{8}$ x $\frac{3}{8}$

References:
Ludwig, *Metalwork Technology and Practice*
Dragoo & Reed, *General Shop Metalwork*
Boyd, *Metalworking*
Smith, *Bench Metalwork*

Procedure:
1. Get out stock for blade.
2. Lay out the holes and center punch.
3. Drill holes to size and countersink back of holes for handle.
4. Finish edges with file.
5. Get out stock for handle (might use $\frac{5}{16}''$ or $\frac{3}{8}''$ round iron and wood handle).
6. Shape ends with file.
7. Lay out the holes and centerpunch.
8. Drill holes.
9. Shape end of handle.
10. Twist handle one turn in center.
11. Assemble handle to blade (handle on top of blade).
12. Finish with emery cloth.

Related Study:
Countersinking
Twisting metal
Riveting

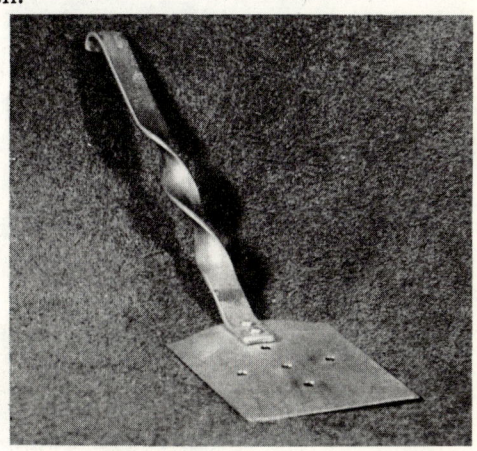

Project 5—Towel Rack

A dish towel rack that will be a practical addition to any kitchen.

Material Required:
1 piece #22 gauge black iron, $2\frac{1}{2}$ x 3
3 pieces #8 galvanized wire, $12\frac{1}{4}$ (or $\frac{3}{16}$ round iron rod)

References:
Ludwig, *Metalwork Technology and Practice*
Dragoo & Reed, *General Shop Metalwork*
Boyd, *Metalworking*

Procedure:
1. Lay out holder and cut to size.
2. Center punch and drill the $\frac{3}{16}$" holes.
3. Bend at right angles on the dotted lines.
4. Align holes.
5. Cut to length, #8 wire $12\frac{1}{4}$" long.
6. Smooth the ends with a file and round corners.
7. Bend to shape in the vise with a hammer.
8. Smooth with emery cloth.
9. Assemble.
10. Finish with emery cloth.
11. Lacquer desired color.

Related Study:
Matching and drilling duplicate holes
Bending
Wire sizes
How sheet iron is made
Laying out a series of holes
Gauges of sheet metal

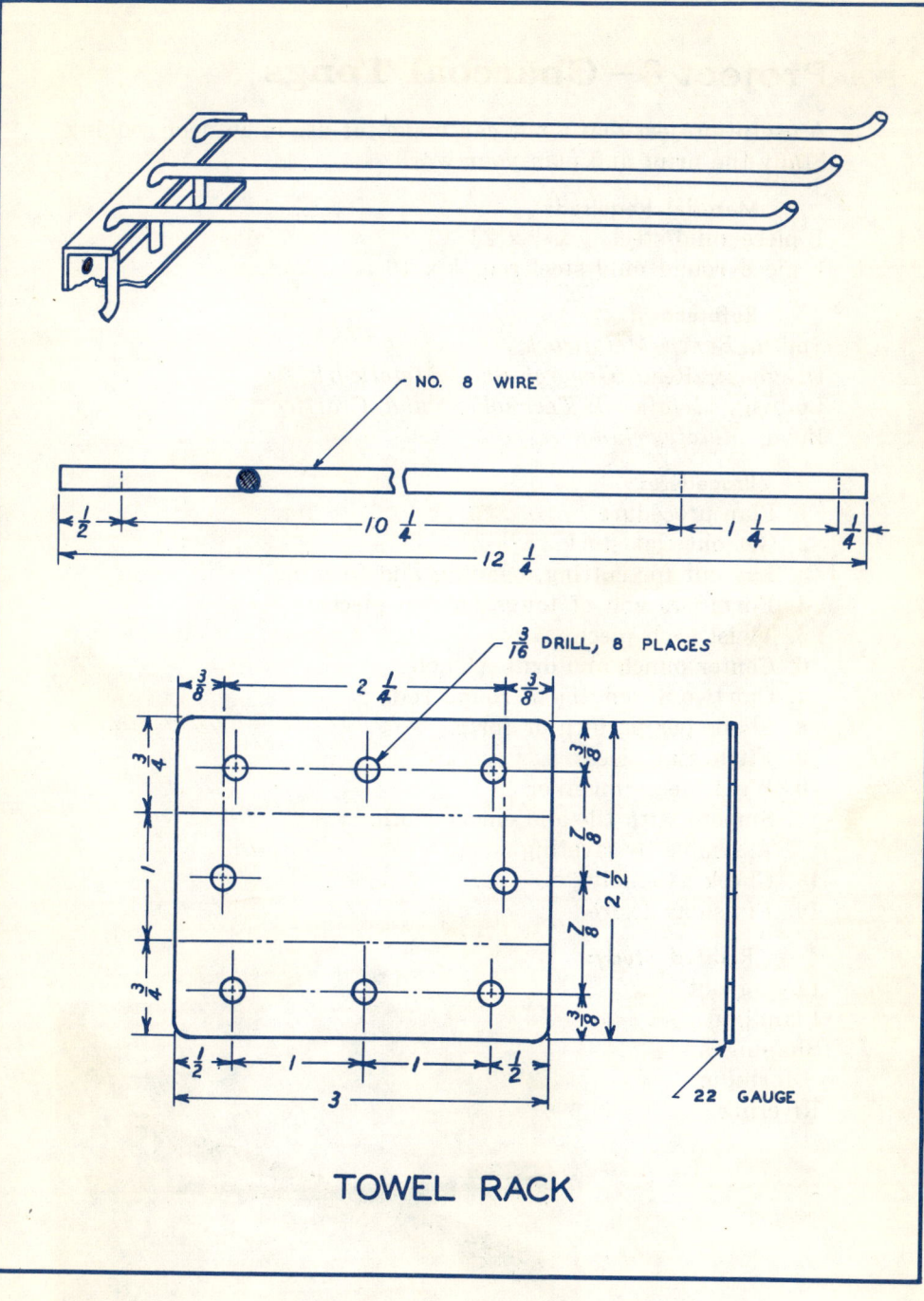

TOWEL RACK

Project 6—Charcoal Tongs

A useful project that a boy can make for use in outdoor cooking. Study the print and plan your work.

Material Required:
1 piece mild steel, $\frac{1}{8}$ x $\frac{1}{2}$ x 24
1 piece round mild steel rod, $\frac{1}{4}$ x 16

References:
Smith, *Bench Metalwork*
Dragoo & Reed, *General Shop Metalwork*
Ludwig, *Metalwork Technology and Practice*
Boyd, *Metalworking*

Procedure:
1. Plan procedure.
2. Get out flat stock.
3. Lay out for cutting, bending and forming.
4. Form cup end of tongs on two pieces.
5. Twist each piece.
6. Center punch and drill $\frac{3}{16}''$ hole.
7. Cut two 8" lengths of round rod.
8. Shape per pattern or form.
9. Fit to flat pieces.
10. Weld pieces together.
11. Smooth with file and emery cloth.
12. Assemble by riveting.
13. Check assembly.
14. Finish as desired.

Related Study:
Laying out
Planning
Shaping and forming
Riveting

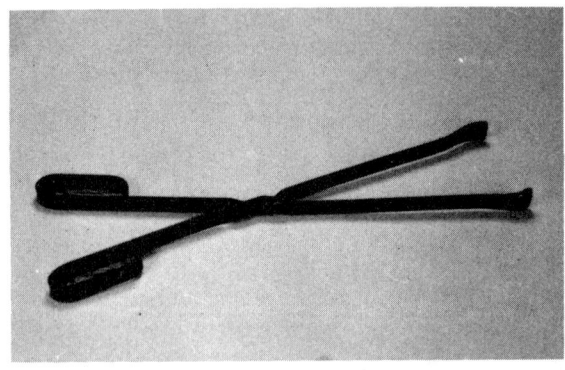

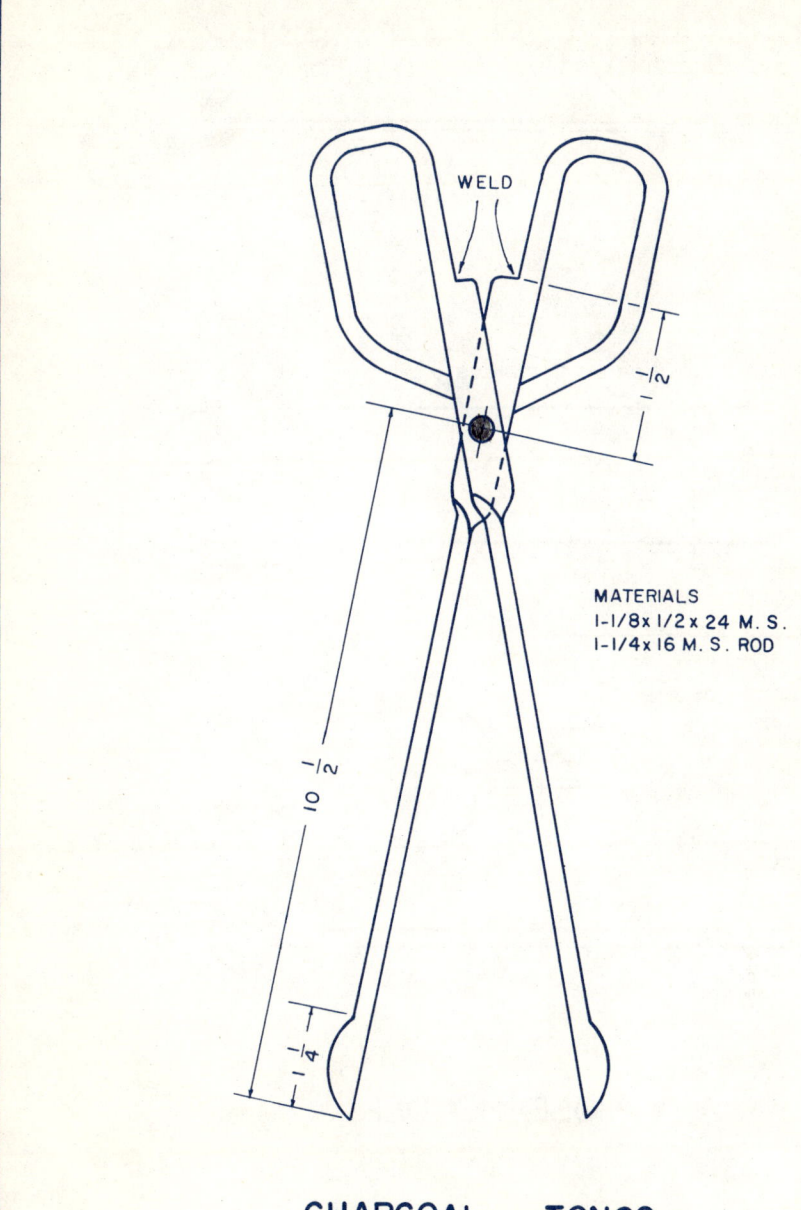

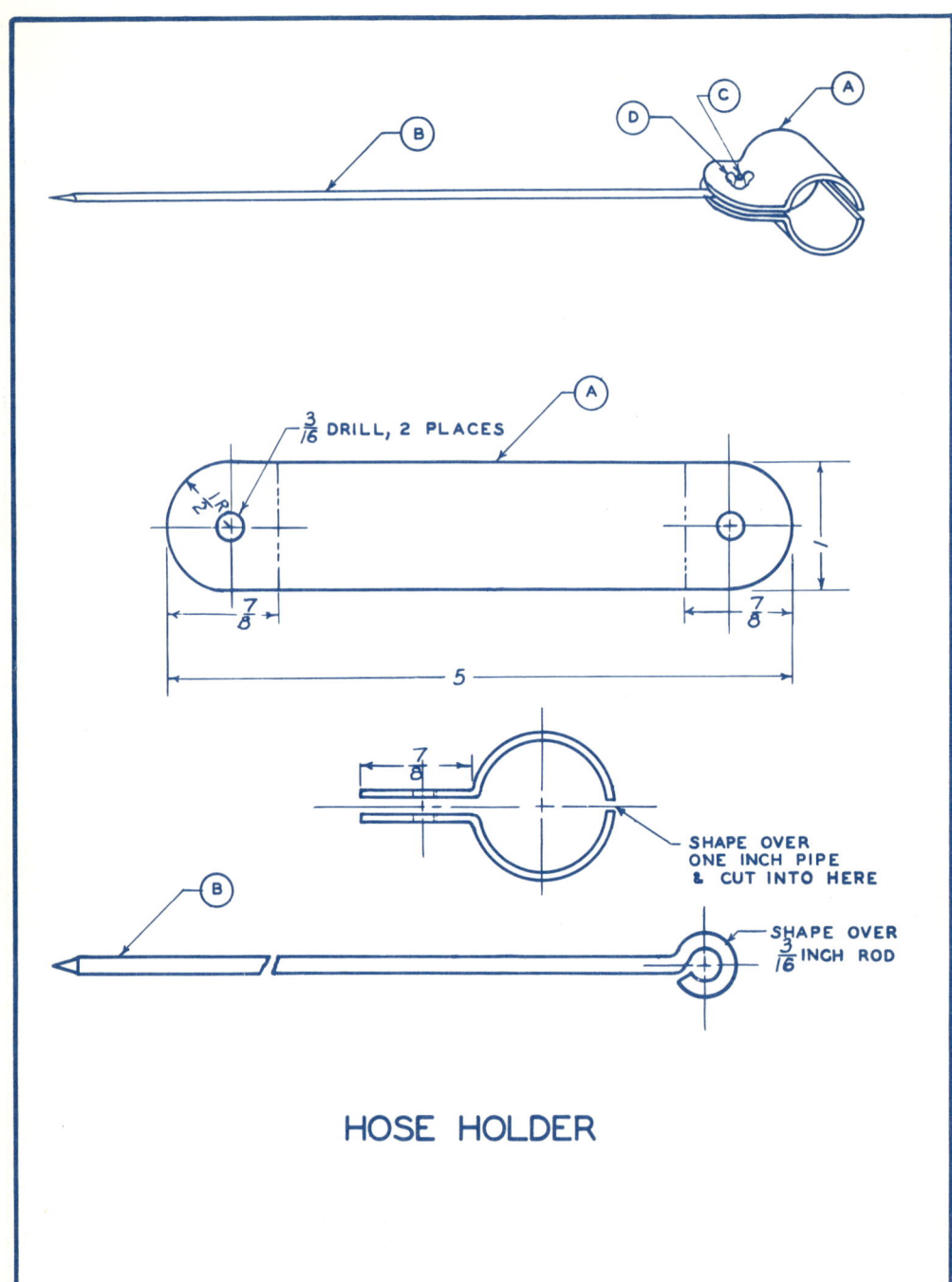

HOSE HOLDER

Project 7—Hose Holder

A handy item for holding the hose in place while sprinkling the lawn or garden.

Material Required:
1 piece round mild steel rod, $\frac{3}{16}$ x 14
1 piece #18 gauge black iron, 1 x 5
1 stove bolt, round head, $\frac{3}{16}$ x $\frac{3}{4}$
1 wing nut, $\frac{3}{16}$

References:
Ludwig, *Metalwork Technology and Practice*
Dragoo & Reed, *General Shop Metalwork*
Boyd, *Metalworking*

Procedure:
1. Get out stock.
2. Lay out holder (A).
3. Cut to size.
4. Drill holes.
5. Shape ends.
6. Finish.
7. Bend to shape over 1" pipe and with vise.
8. Cut through center, as shown.
9. Smooth with file.
10. Get out rod for upright.
11. Heat and shape eye.
12. File end for point.
13. Assemble.
14. Check.
15. Paint or finish as desired.

Related Study:
Fasteners
Gauges and sizes of sheet metal
Safety in drilling sheet metal
Making an eye

Project 8—Garden Trowel

A useful flower garden tool that will delight any mother. The trowel is strong and sturdy and will last a long time.

Material Required:
1 piece #18 gauge black iron, 4 x $6\frac{3}{4}$
1 piece band iron, $\frac{1}{8}$ x $\frac{3}{4}$ x 9 or $\frac{3}{16}$ x $\frac{3}{4}$ x 9
2 handles (aluminum), $\frac{1}{4}$ x $\frac{3}{4}$ x 4
2 rivets, soft iron or aluminum, $\frac{3}{16}$ x $\frac{3}{4}$
2 rivets, soft iron, round head, $\frac{3}{16}$ x $\frac{3}{8}$

References:
Ludwig, *Metalwork Technology and Practice*
Dragoo & Reed, *General Shop Metalwork*
Smith, *Bench Metalwork*

Procedure:
1. Lay out pattern for blade on heavy paper.
2. Transfer pattern to metal with scriber.
3. Cut to shape.
4. File edges smooth and sharpen end of blade.
5. Shape blade.
6. Get out stock for handle.
7. Lay out.
8. Drill holes.
9. Shape end.
10. Shape handle as shown.
11. Cut aluminum strips for handle.
12. Drill holes to fit handle.
13. Countersink holes in handle.
14. Rivet to main handle.
15. File each side smooth.
16. Rivet blade to handle (handle on top of blade).
17. Finish with emery cloth.
18. Paint desired color.

Related Study:
Rivets
Proper practices in riveting
Patterns
Cutting heavy gauge metal

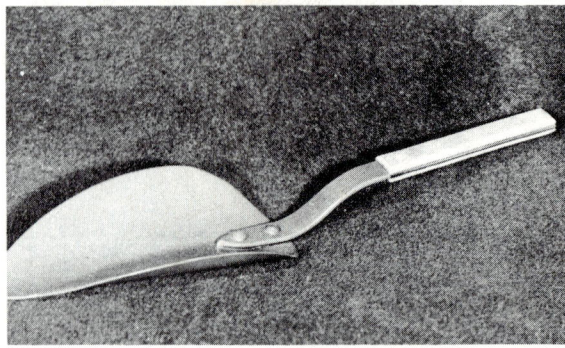

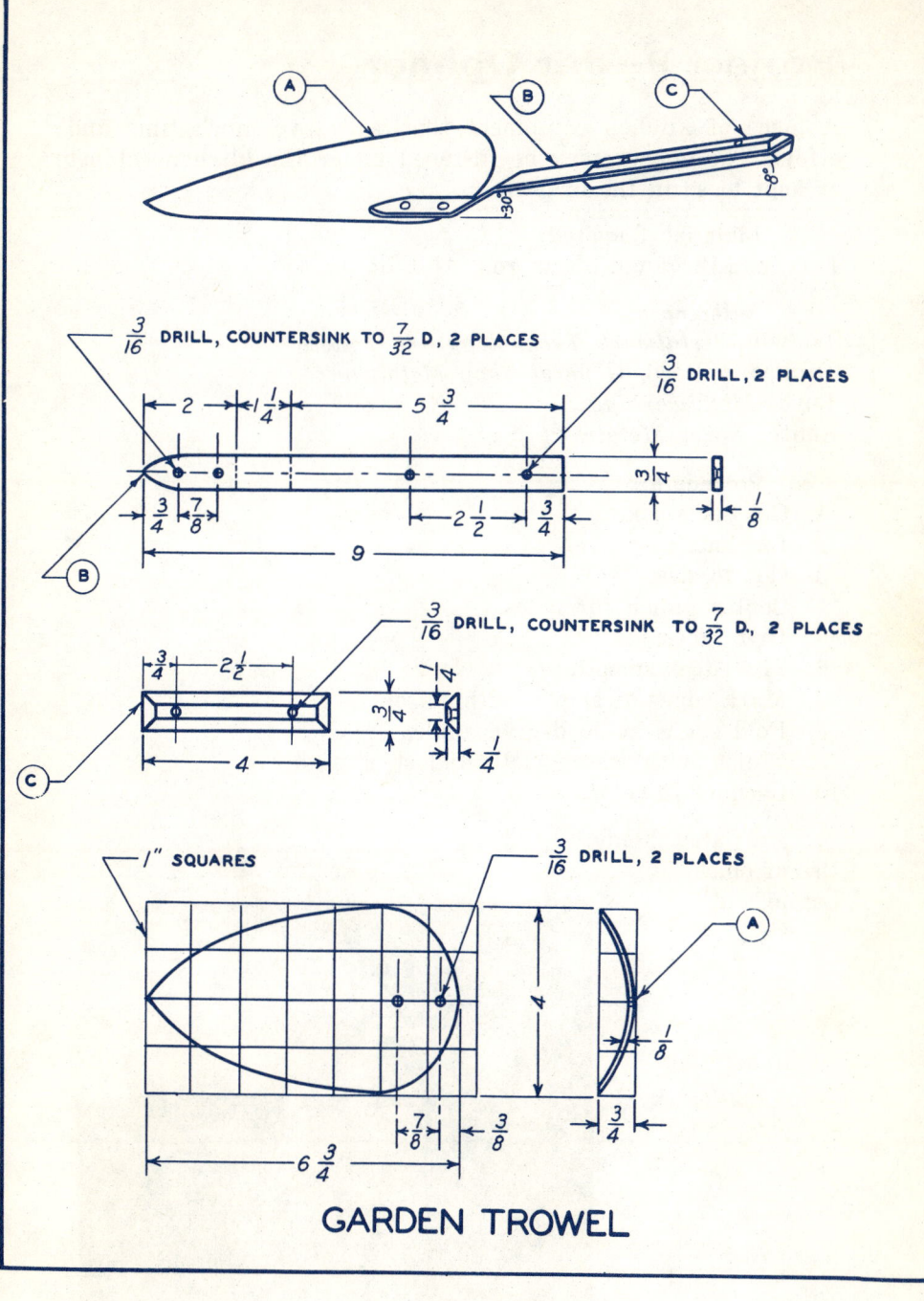

Project 9—Jar Opener

A piece of kitchen equipment that will save much time and effort. The opener may be fastened under the kitchen cabinet or kept loose in the drawer.

Material Required:
1 piece #18 gauge black iron, $4\frac{1}{2}$ x 6

References:
Ludwig, *Metalwork Technology and Practice*
Dragoo & Reed, *General Shop Metalwork*
Boyd, *Metalworking*
Smith, *Sheet Metalwork*

Procedure:
1. Get out stock.
2. Lay out.
3. Cut to size.
4. Center punch for holes.
5. Drill holes.
6. File edges smooth.
7. Mark edges as shown with chisel.
8. Fold edges at 90 degree angle.
9. Finish with emery cloth and steel wool.
10. Lacquer in color.

Related Study:
Use of chisel
Laying out

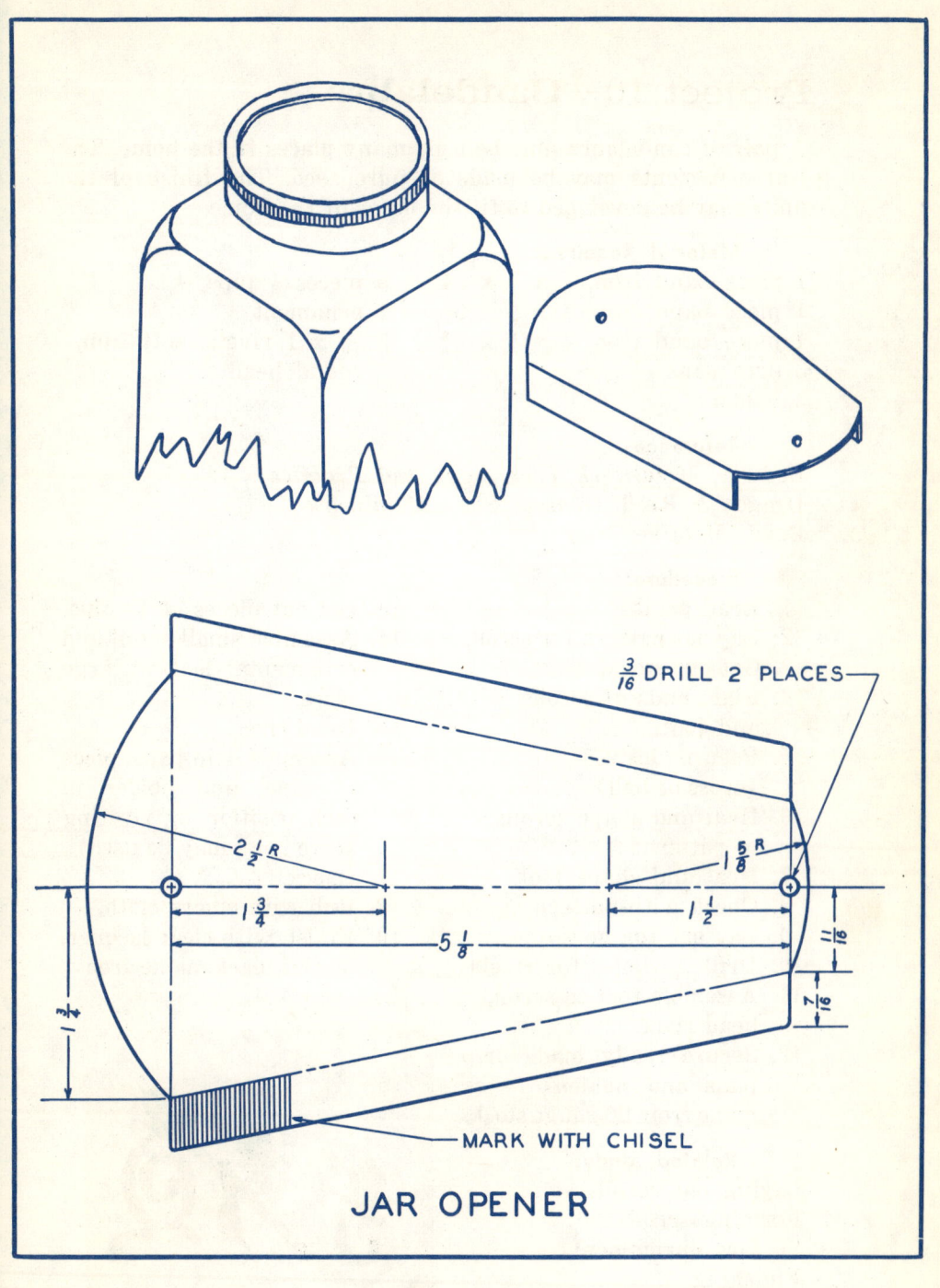

Project 10—Candelabra

A pair of candelabra may be used many places in the home. The leaf ornaments may be made or purchased. The finish of the units may be developed to fit the decor of the home.

Material Required:

1 piece band iron, $\frac{1}{8}$ x $\frac{3}{4}$ x 34
1 piece band iron, $\frac{1}{8}$ x $\frac{3}{4}$ x 6
1 piece band iron, $\frac{1}{8}$ x $\frac{3}{4}$ x $4\frac{3}{4}$
3 drip pans
3 holders
3 pieces $\frac{1}{8}$ pipe, $\frac{1}{2}$
1 ornament
5 $\frac{3}{16}$ x 1 rivets, soft iron, round head

References:

Ludwig, *Metalwork Technology and Practice*
Dragoo & Reed, *General Shop Metalwork*
Boyd, *Metalworking*

Procedure:

1. Read print.
2. Lay out pattern for scroll.
3. Get out stock.
4. Flare ends of scrolls and foot.
5. Peen if desired (cross or ball).
6. Heat and shape scrolls to pattern.
7. Heat and shape foot.
8. Check with pattern.
9. Lay out for holes.
10. Drill $\frac{3}{16}''$ holes for rivets.
11. Assemble foot to scroll, head rivet.
12. Secure ready made drip pans and holders — or make from 26 gauge stock.
13. Get out pieces of $\frac{1}{8}''$ pipe.
14. Assemble small scroll and ornamental leaf to large piece.
15. Head rivet.
16. Assemble drip pans, piece of pipe, and holder in each position by riveting stove bolts may be used).
17. Check.
18. Rub with emery cloth.
19. Finish with clear lacquer, or flat black, as desired.

Related Study:

Laying out scrolls
Forming scrolls
Surface enrichment
Finishing

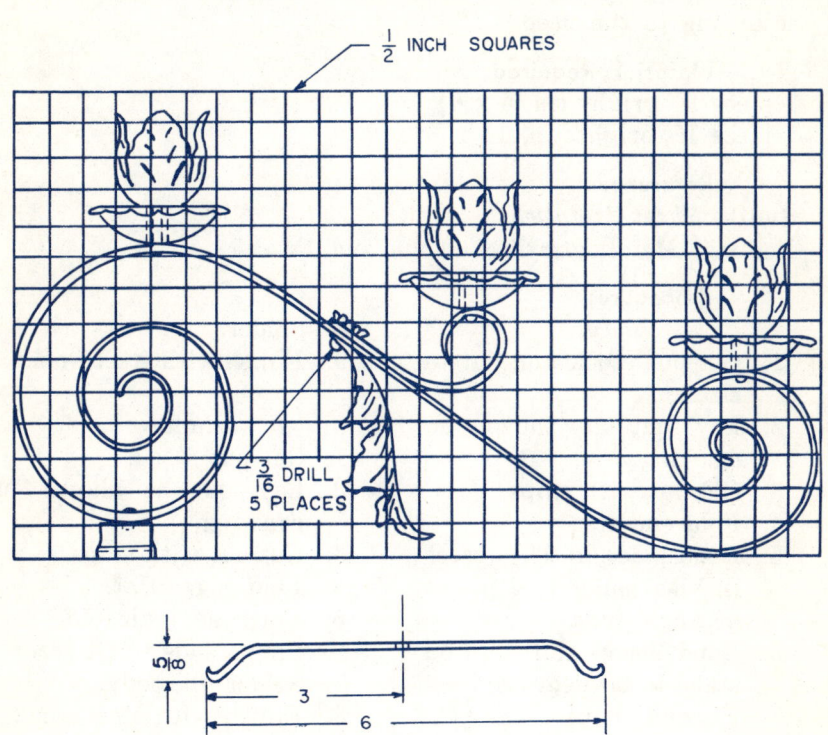

CANDELABRA

Project 11—Scoop

A scoop with many uses. The size and design may be varied according to the need.

Material Required:
1 piece IC bright tin, 5 x $6\frac{1}{4}$
1 piece IC bright tin, $1\frac{1}{4}$ x $3\frac{3}{4}$

References:
Smith, *Sheet Metalwork*
Ludwig, *Metalwork Technology and Practice*

Procedure:

Body:
1. Get out stock and cut to size.
2. Lay out as shown on drawing.
3. Cut out with snips.
4. Fold end flat.
5. Bend sides to 90 degrees in vise using two pieces of angle iron.
6. Bend back and top on stake to 90 degrees.
7. Fit and shape.
8. Solder.
9. Finish with steel wool.

Handle:
1. Get out stock.
2. Lay out as shown on drawing.
3. Cut out with snips.
4. Fold edges flat.
5. Form as indicated.
6. Shape ends to fit scoop.
7. Solder to body.
8. Finish with steel wool.

Related Study:
Composition and melting temperature of solder
Sheet metal tools and equipment
Kinds of stakes
Soldering
Use of bar folder
Steel wool

PAGE 30

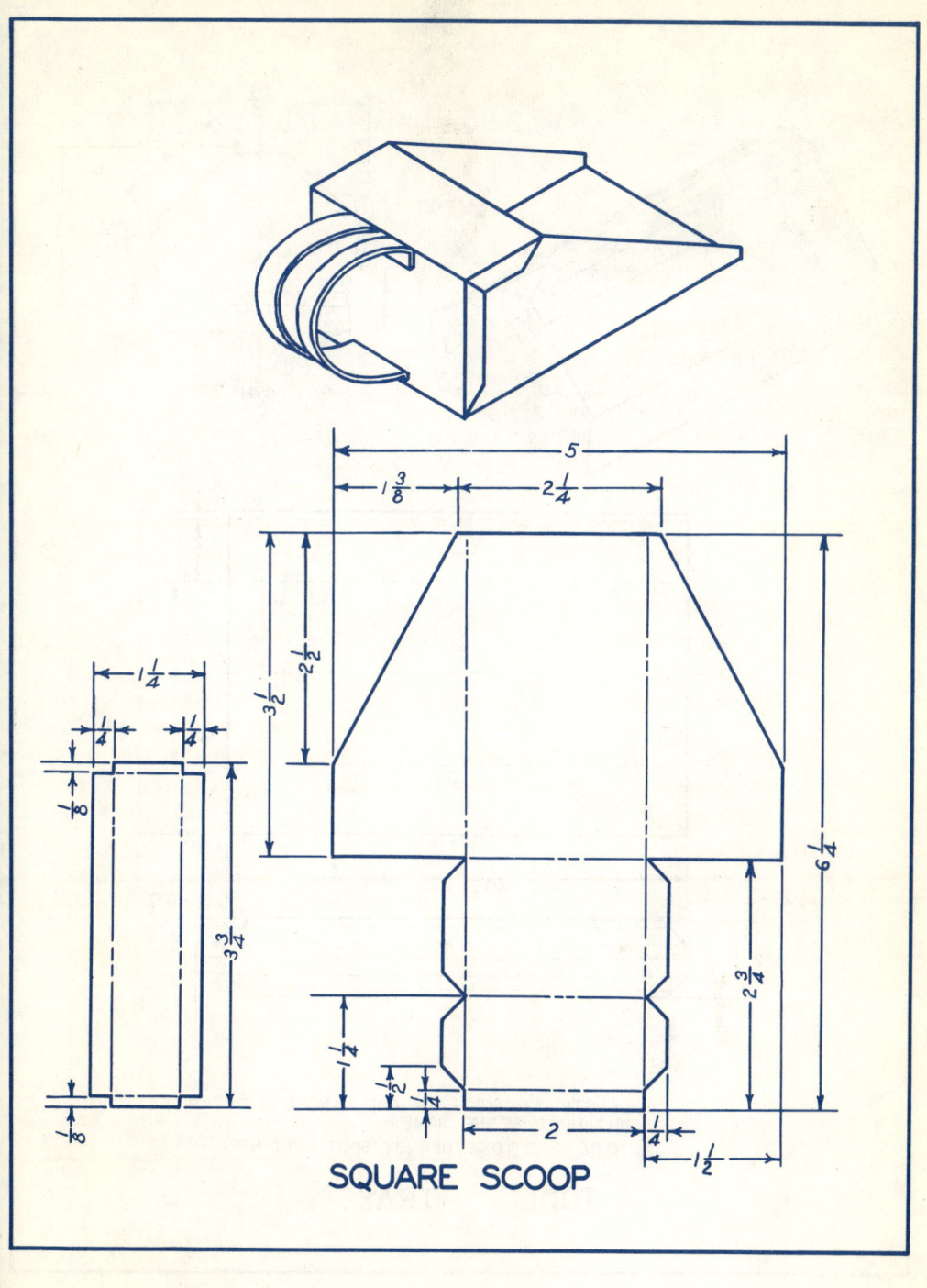

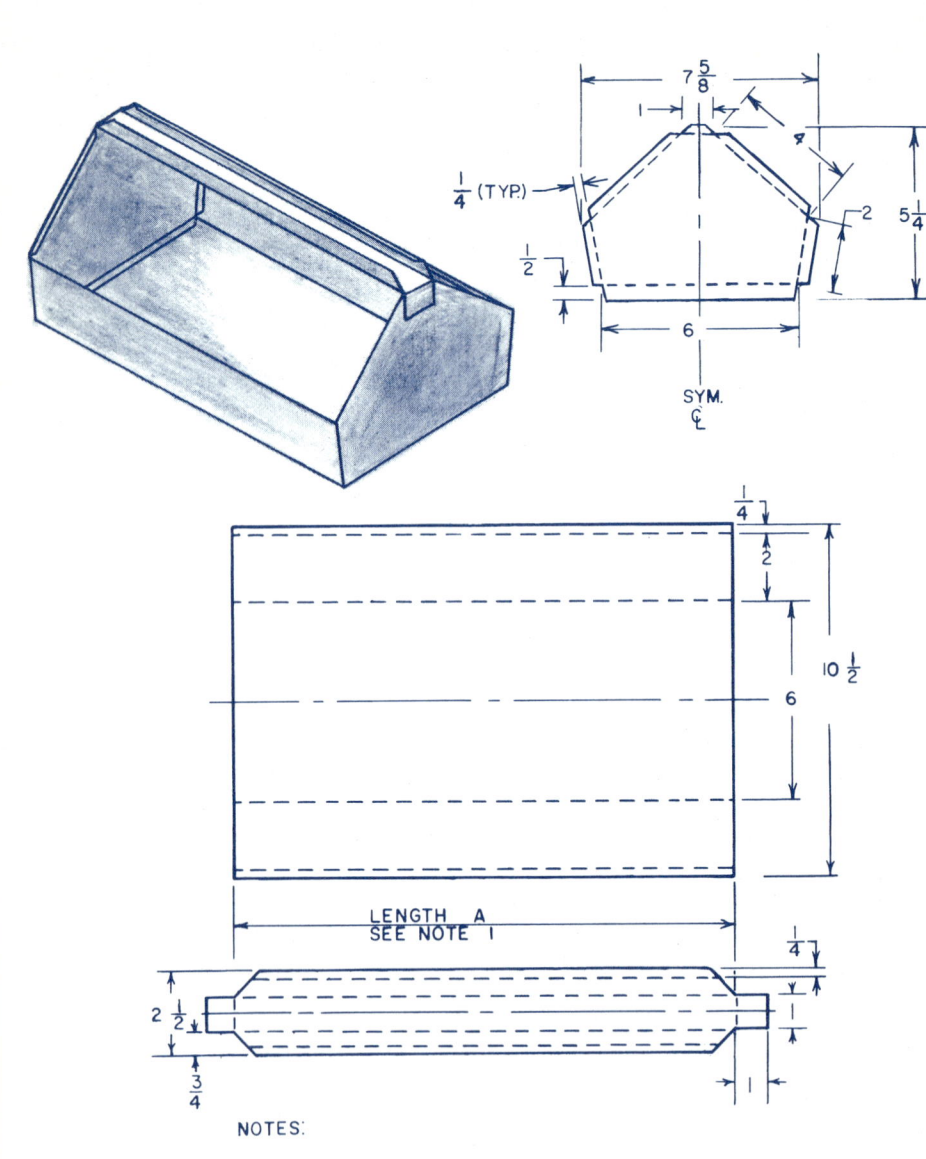

NOTES:
1. LENGTH (A) OF BOTTOM AND HANDLE IS OPTIONAL BUT MUST BE THE SAME.
2. TO BE HELD TOGETHER BY SPOT WELDING

TOOL TRAY

Project 12—Tool Tray

This handy tray may be used in the home workshop. Fundamental sheet metal processes are involved, so the tool tray may be used as a line production product. Assemble by riveting, soldering, or spot welding.

Material Required:
2 pieces #28 gauge galvanized iron, $5\frac{1}{4}$ x $7\frac{5}{8}$
1 piece #28 gauge galvanized iron, $10\frac{1}{2}$ x length (optional)
1 piece #22 gauge galvanized iron, $2\frac{1}{2}$ x length plus 2

References:
Smith, *Sheet Metalwork*
Dragoo & Reed, *General Shop Metalwork*
Ludwig, *Metalwork Technology and Practice*
Feirer & Lindbeck, *Industrial Arts Metalwork*

Procedure:
1. Lay out pattern.
2. Get out stock.
3. Lay out for bends.
4. Check layout.
5. Cut ends and bottom section, with snips.
6. Fold ends, per print.
7. Fold bottom and sides. Note hems and right angle bends.
8. Fold and shape handle.
9. Check parts with pattern and print.
10. Fit and assemble parts.
11. Hold parts together with clamps.
12. Spot weld all joints.
13. Check unit.
14. Smooth and clean.
15. Finish if desired.

Related Study:
Laying out
Bending
Fitting
Spot Welding
Riveting
Soldering

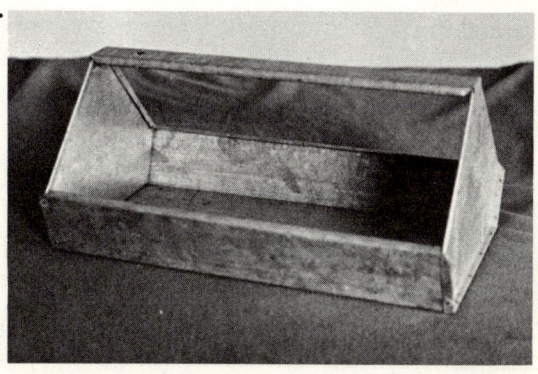

Project 13—Spice Rack

A spice rack to fasten on the inside door of the kitchen cabinet. The size may be adjusted to meet particular requirements.

Material Required:
1 piece aluminum, .032 x 7¾ x 12
1 piece aluminum, .032 x ½ x 16¾
2 rivets, aluminum, oval head, ⅛ x ¼

References:
Ludwig, *Metalwork Technology and Practice*
Smith, *Sheet Metalwork*
Boyd, *Metalworking*

Procedure:
1. Read print.
2. Get out stock.
3. Lay out to size.
4. Cut to size.
5. Lay out radius.
6. Cut to shape.
7. Lay out and drill holes.
8. Countersink back of holes, back piece.
9. Finish pieces.
10. Lay out for bending.
11. Bend.
12. Assemble pieces by riveting.
13. Finish.

Related Study:
Bend allowance
Bending
Finishing aluminum
Gauges of aluminum

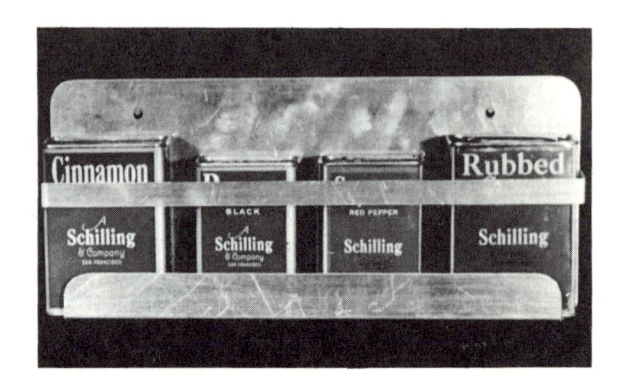

SPICE RACK

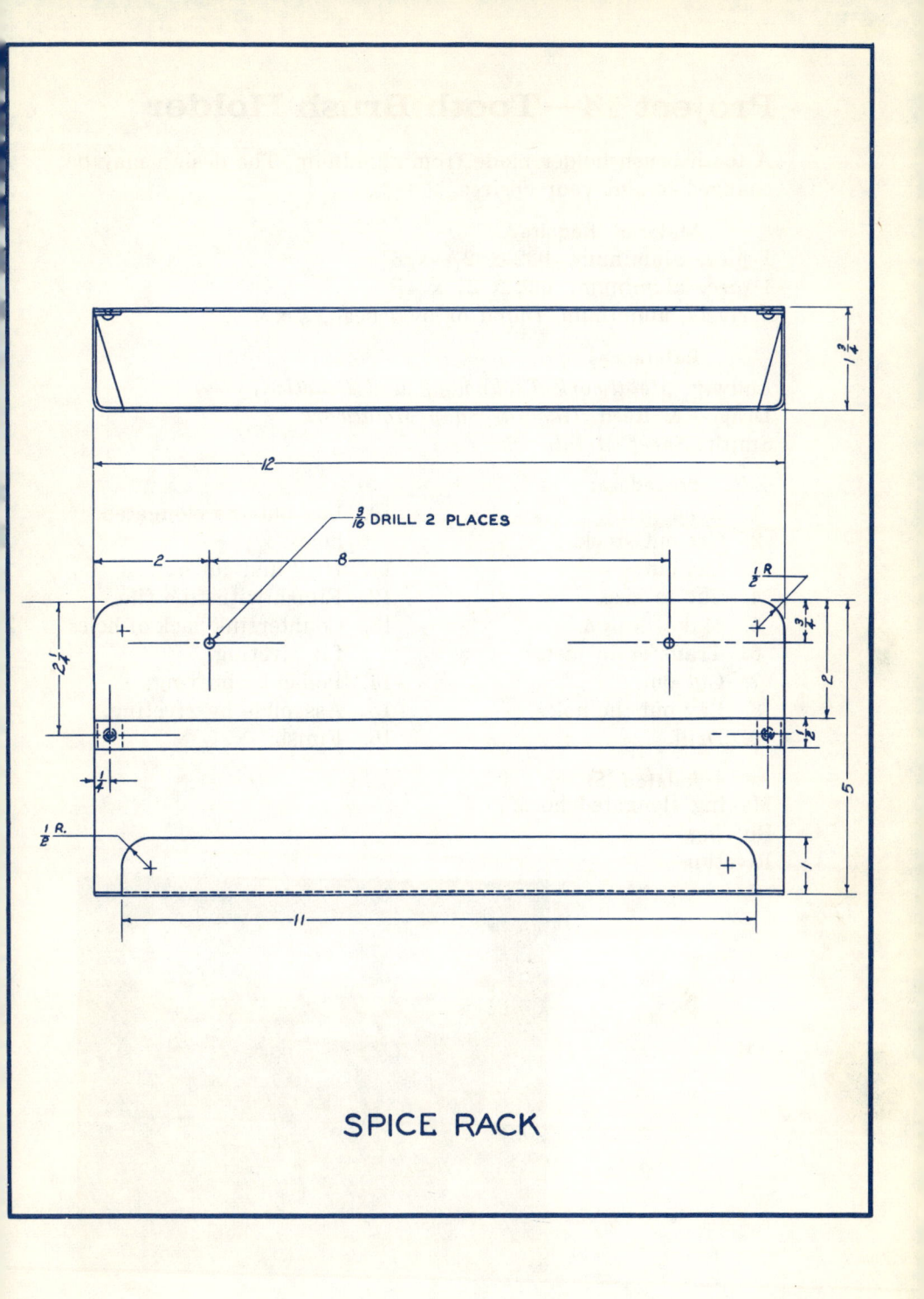

Project 14—Tooth Brush Holder

A tooth brush holder made from aluminum. The design may be changed to suit your desires.

Material Required:
1 piece aluminum, .032 x $2\frac{5}{16}$ x 6
1 piece aluminum, .032 x $2\frac{1}{4}$ x $4\frac{1}{2}$
6 rivets, aluminum, round or oval head, $\frac{1}{8}$ x $\frac{1}{4}$

References:
Ludwig, *Metalwork Technology and Practice*
Dragoo & Reed, *General Shop Metalwork*
Smith, *Sheet Metalwork*

Procedure:
1. Read print.
2. Get out stock.
3. Lay out.
4. Cut to size.
5. Make design.
6. Transfer to metal.
7. Cut out.
8. Lay out the holes.
9. Drill.
10. Lay out the elongated holes.
11. Drill and cut out.
12. Finish with fine file.
13. Countersink back of holes for riveting.
14. Polish by buffing.
15. Assemble by riveting.
16. Finish.

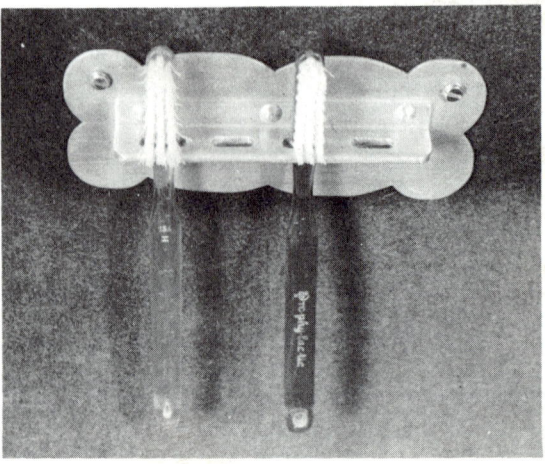

Related Study:
Making elongated holes
Buffing
Riveting

TOOTH BRUSH HOLDER

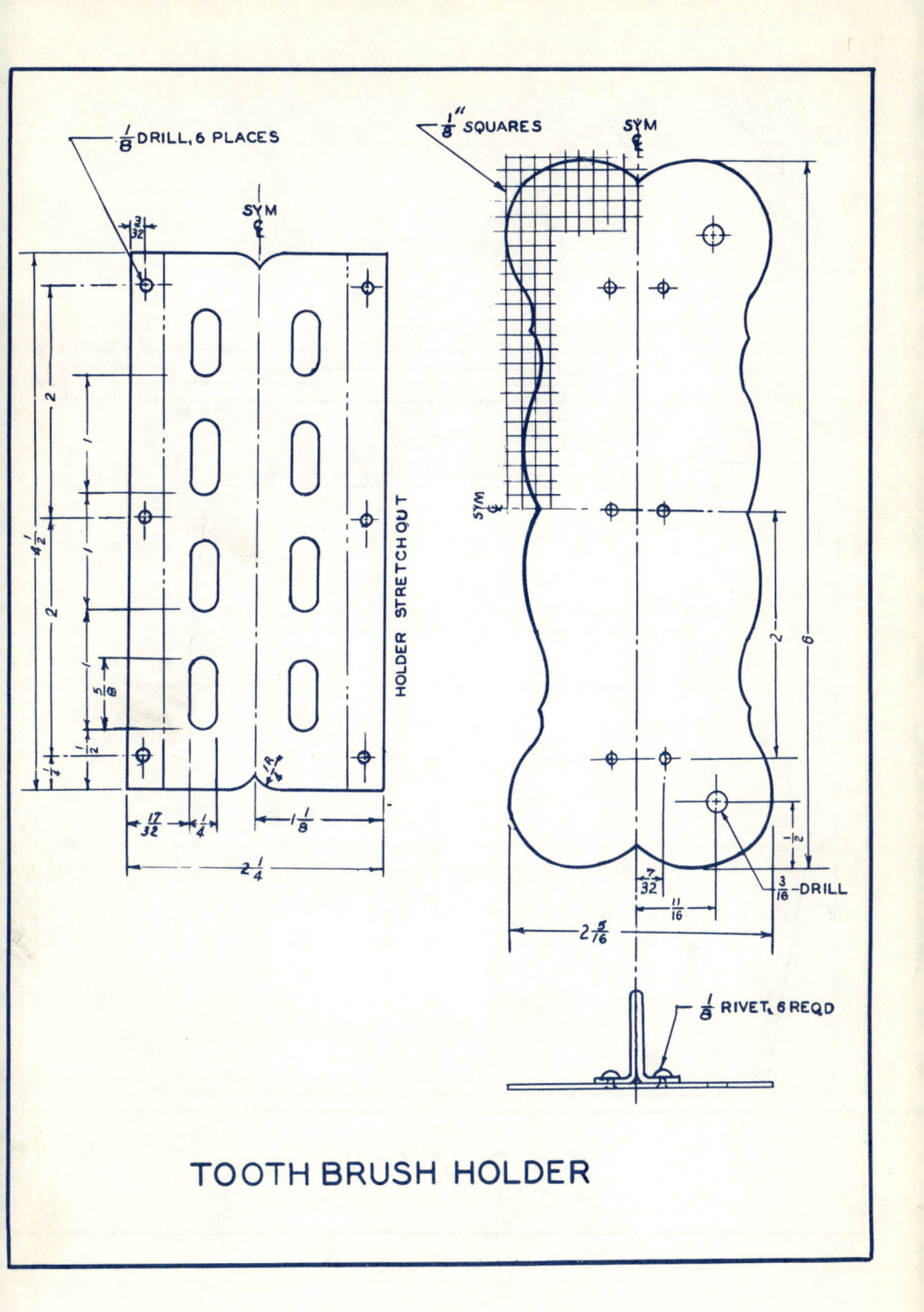

DUST PAN

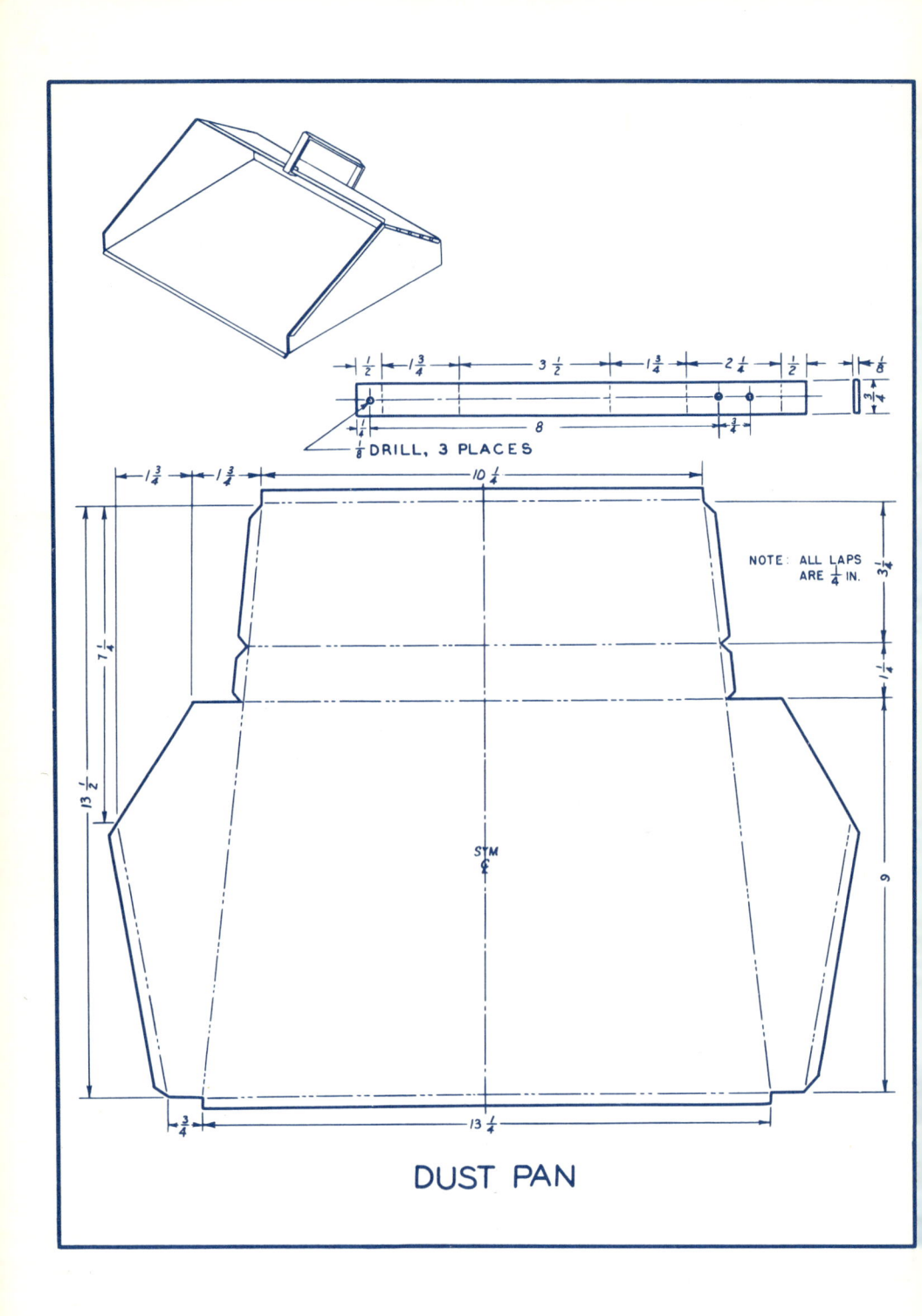

Project 15—Dust Pan

A practical project that will give good service. The handle is shaped so that when the pan is resting on the floor the back piece of the handle elevates at the correct angle.

Material Required:
1 piece #26 gauge galvanized iron, $14\frac{1}{2}$ x $17\frac{3}{4}$
1 piece band iron, $\frac{1}{8}$ x $\frac{3}{4}$ x $10\frac{1}{4}$
4 rivets, tinner's 1 lb.
3 rivets, S.I., R.H., $\frac{3}{16}$ x $\frac{3}{4}$

References:
Ludwig, *Metalwork Technology and Practice*
Dragoo & Reed, *General Shop Metalwork*

Procedure:
1. Get out stock; cut to size.
2. Lay out.
3. Cut to shape.
4. Hem edges as shown.
5. Bend sides up.
6. Bend back and top.
7. Check.
8. Clamp and center punch for rivet holes.
9. Drill $\frac{1}{8}$" hole.
10. Rivet with tinner's rivets.
11. Solder joints if desired.
12. Get out stock for handle.
13. Lay out as shown.
14. Center punch and drill $\frac{3}{16}$" holes for riveting in place.
15. Shape handle as shown and bend end of handle for foot.
16. Check and mark for holes in dust pan.
17. Drill holes for handle.
18. Rivet handle in place.
19. Check.
20. Smooth with steel wool and emery cloth.
21. Paint, if desired.

Related Study:
Tinner's rivets
Heading rivets
Bending a hem
Braking sheet metal
Steel wool, and its use

Project 16—Memo Pad Holder

The size of this memo pad holder may be changed to fit the size of paper desired. It is useful in the office or kitchen. Brass bolts may be used in place of stove bolts. Felt strips on feet of holder will keep it from scratching the desk top.

Material Required:
1 piece aluminum, .051 x $4\frac{1}{16}$ x $8\frac{1}{2}$
1 piece aluminum, .051 x $\frac{1}{2}$ x $4\frac{1}{16}$
2 stove bolts, R. H., $\frac{3}{16}$ x 1
1 memo pad, 4 x 6

References:
Ludwig, *Metalwork Technology and Practice*
Dragoo & Reed, *General Shop Metalwork*
Smith, *Sheet Metalwork*

Procedure:
1. Get out stock for holder and top strip.
2. Smooth edges.
3. Lay out the holes.
4. Lay out the bends.
5. Drill $\frac{3}{16}$" holes.
6. Make bends.
7. Polish pieces with buffer.
8. Drill or punch holes in paper pad.
9. Assemble pad, holder and top strip.

Related Study:
Bend allowance
Filing aluminum
Buffing

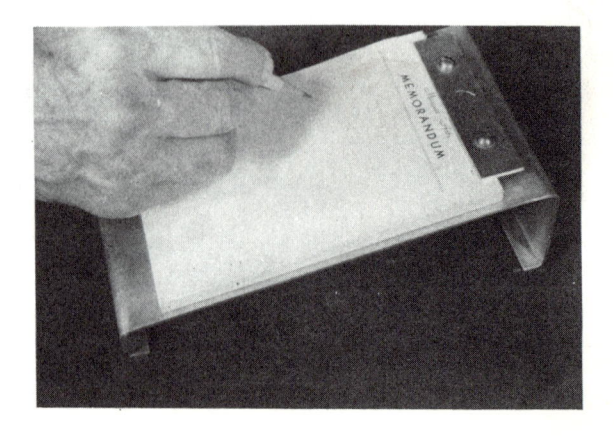

MEMO PAD HOLDER

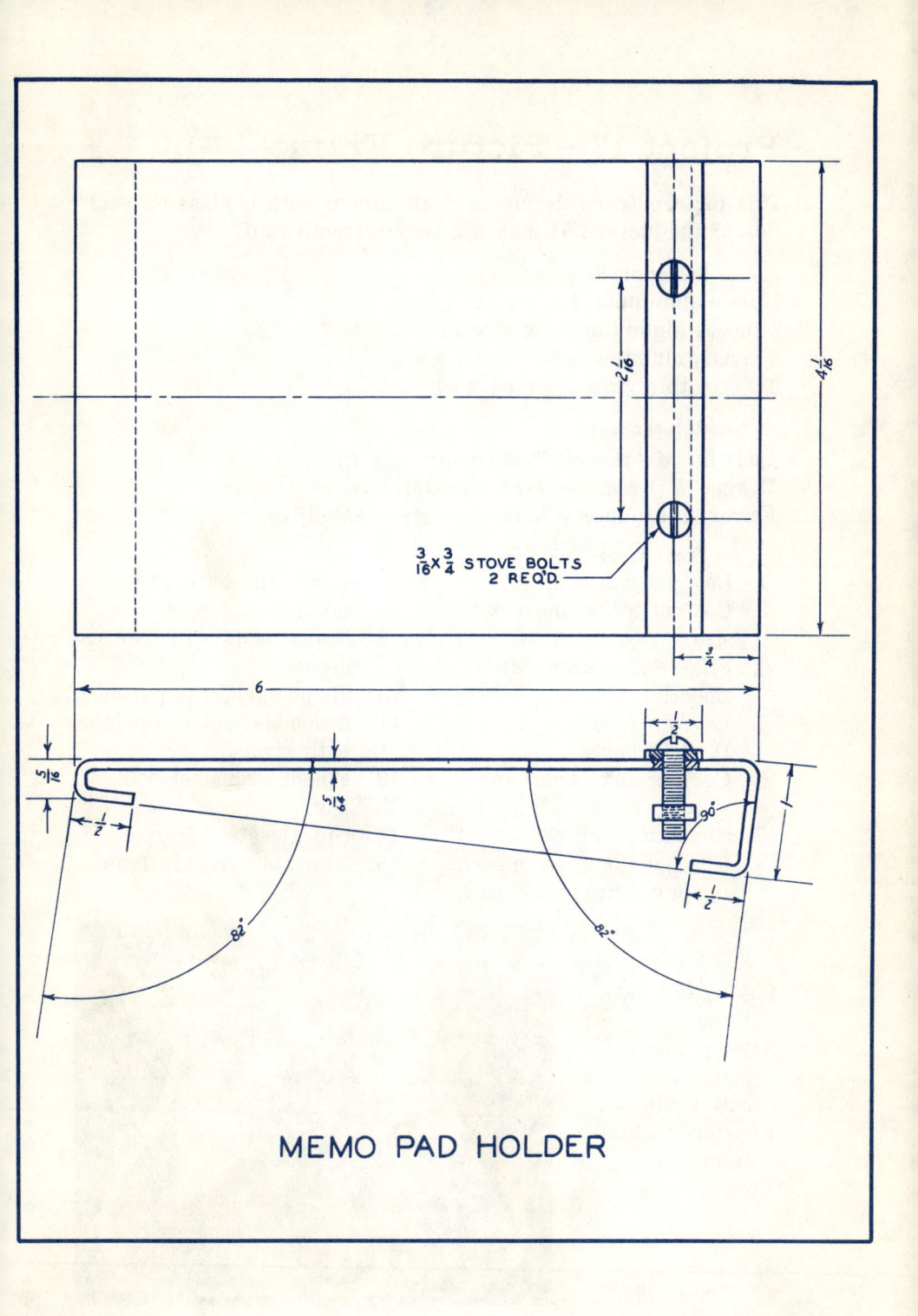

Project 17—Picture Frame

This picture frame is made of aluminum with a glass on each side of the picture. It makes a very attractive gift.

Material Required:
1 piece aluminum, $\frac{1}{8}$ x $\frac{1}{2}$ x 12
2 pieces aluminum, $\frac{1}{8}$ x $\frac{1}{2}$ x $1\frac{1}{4}$
2 rivets, aluminum, 82° ctsk., $\frac{1}{8}$ x $\frac{3}{8}$
2 pieces thin glass, $\frac{1}{16}$ x $3\frac{1}{4}$ x $4\frac{1}{4}$

References:
Ludwig, *Metalwork Technology and Practice*
Dragoo & Reed, *General Shop Metalwork*
Feirer & Lindbeck, *Industrial Arts Metalwork*

Procedure:
1. Lay out pattern.
2. Get out stock and cut to size.
3. File ends even and smooth.
4. Lay out holes.
5. Drill $\frac{1}{8}''$ holes.
6. Countersink holes as shown.
7. Shape top curves.
8. Cut slot for glass in each upright with hack saw. (Use three blades on saw.)
9. Finish slots with file as needed.
10. Shape upright to pattern.
11. Assemble feet to upright with rivets.
12. Finish with steel wool.
13. Buff.
14. Cut glass for frame.
15. Assemble glass in frame.

Related Study:
Laying out patterns
Sawing with more than one saw blade
Polishing aluminum
Cutting glass

PICTURE FRAME

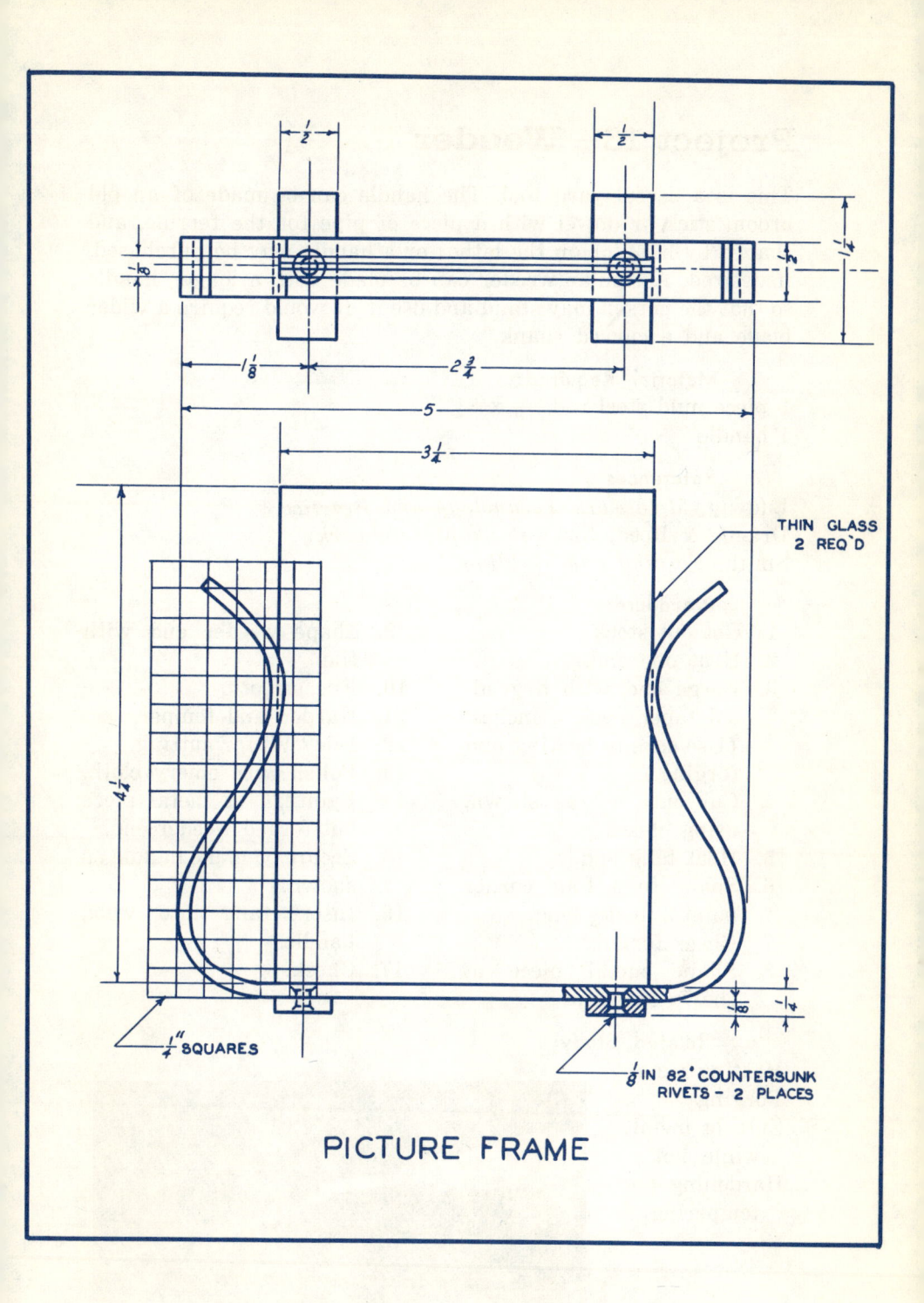

Project 18 — Weeder

This is a useful yard tool. The handle can be made of an old broom stick or dowel with a piece of pipe for the ferrule, and shaped by hand or on the lathe; or a handle may be purchased, if desired. A similar weeder can be made with a longer handle so that the person may stand and use it. It would require a wider blade and a curved shank.

Material Required:
1 piece mild steel rod, $\frac{5}{16}$ x $8\frac{1}{2}$
1 handle

References:
Ludwig, *Metalwork Technology and Practice*
Dragoo & Reed, *General Shop Metalwork*
Smith, *Forging and Welding*

Procedure:
1. Get out stock.
2. Heat one end.
3. Forge end with a gradual taper back 4 inches. (Use care in heating and forging.)
4. Cut out "V" as shown, using chisel.
5. Heat tang end.
6. Shape to a four corner point 2 inches long.
7. Check forging.
8. Shape metal piece as shown on print.
9. Shape weeder end with file.
10. File smooth.
11. Harden and temper.
12. File "V" for cutting.
13. Polish with emery cloth.
14. Paint all of metal piece but forged weeder end.
15. Secure or make handle as shown.
16. Insert tang into wood handle.
17. Check.

Related Study:
Heating metal
Forging
Cutting metal while hot
Hardening and tempering

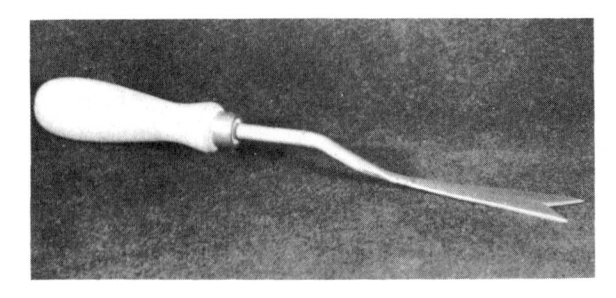

WEEDER

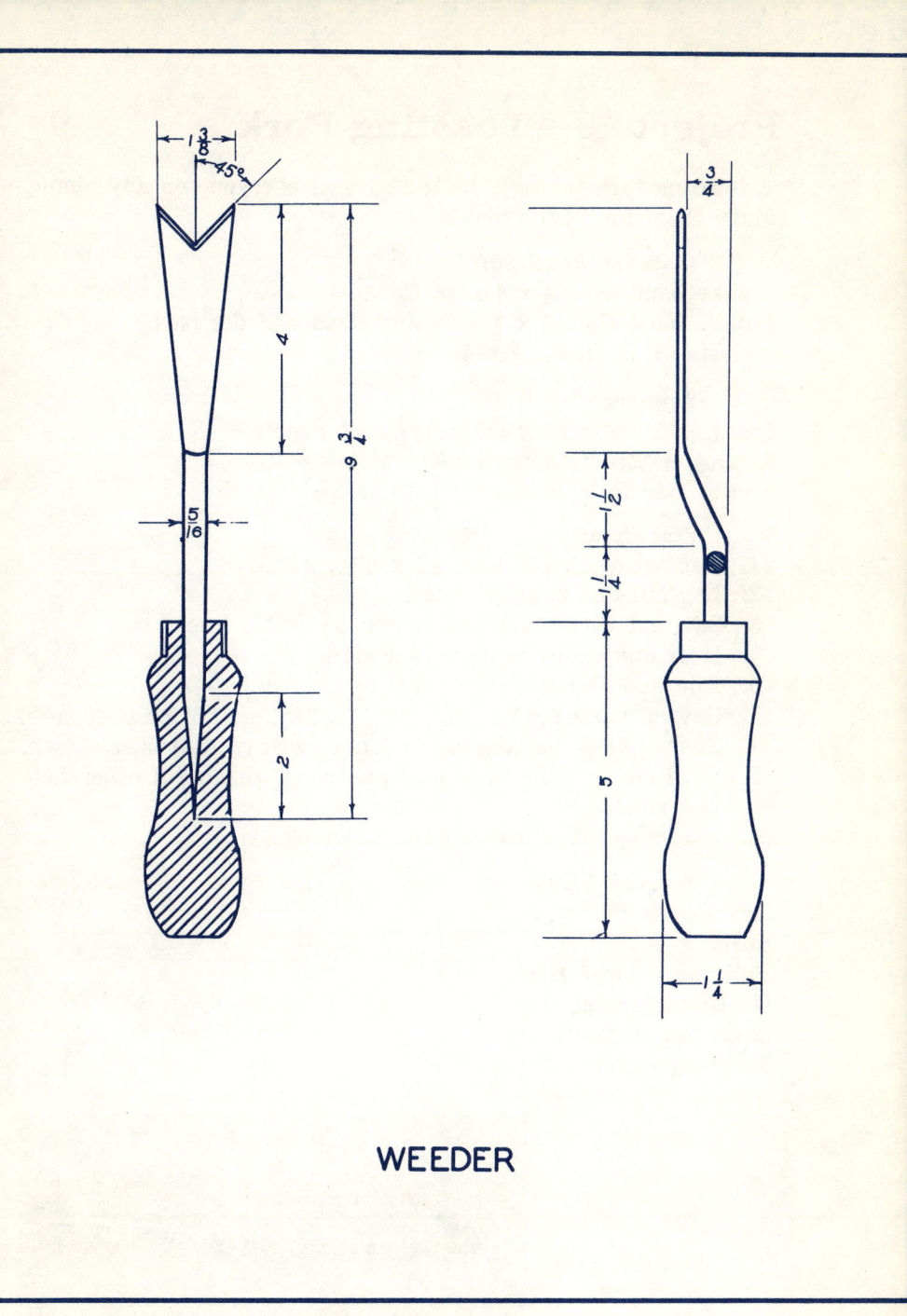

Project 19—Toasting Fork

A toasting fork that will be the envy of everyone on any picnic. Make them for your friends.

Material Required:
1 piece band iron, $\frac{1}{8}$ x $\frac{3}{4}$ x $4\frac{1}{2}$
1 piece band iron, $\frac{1}{8}$ x $\frac{3}{8}$ x 36 (or shorter if desired)
2 rivets, S. I., R. H., $\frac{1}{8}$ x $\frac{1}{2}$

References:
Ludwig, *Metalwork Technology and Practice*
Dragoo & Reed, *General Shop Metalwork*
Smith, *Bench Metalwork*

Procedure:
1. Get out stock for fork $\frac{1}{8}$" x $\frac{3}{4}$" x $4\frac{1}{2}$"
2. Lay out and drill $\frac{1}{8}$" holes.
3. Saw out waste stock as shown on dotted lines.
4. Heat and shape to desired design.
5. File and finish.
6. Get out stock for handle $\frac{1}{8}$" x $\frac{3}{8}$" x 36", or shorter if desired.
7. Shape handle on bending fork and twist two turns as shown.
8. Drill one $\frac{1}{8}$" hole in handle and rivet, then drill other hole and rivet.
9. Assemble and finish. (Head all rivets.)

Related Study:
Hot forming
Forging
Building a forge fire
Heating of metal
Operating a gas forge
Twisting metal

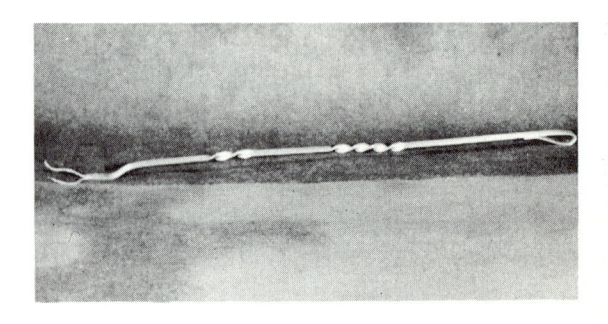

FORK

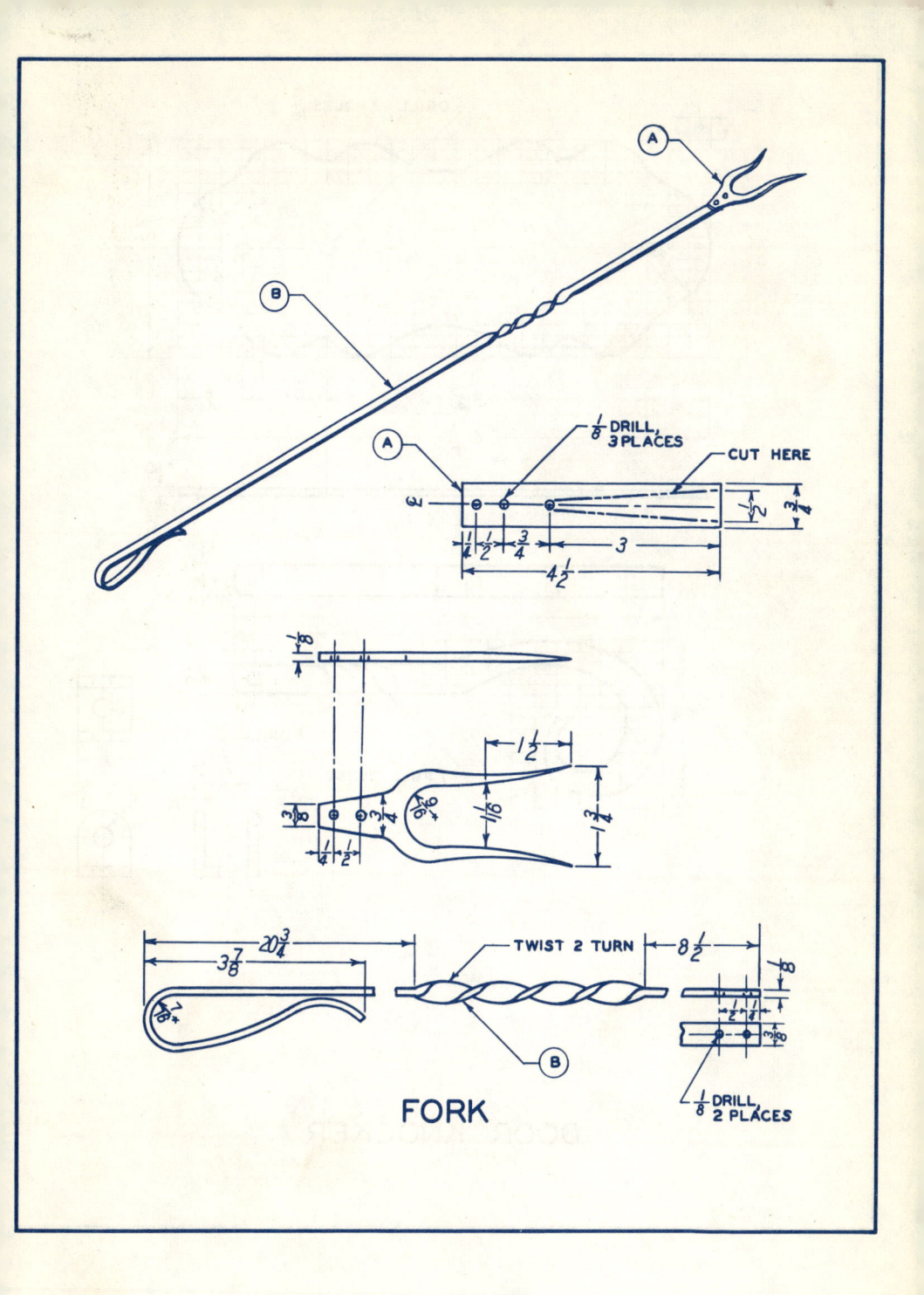

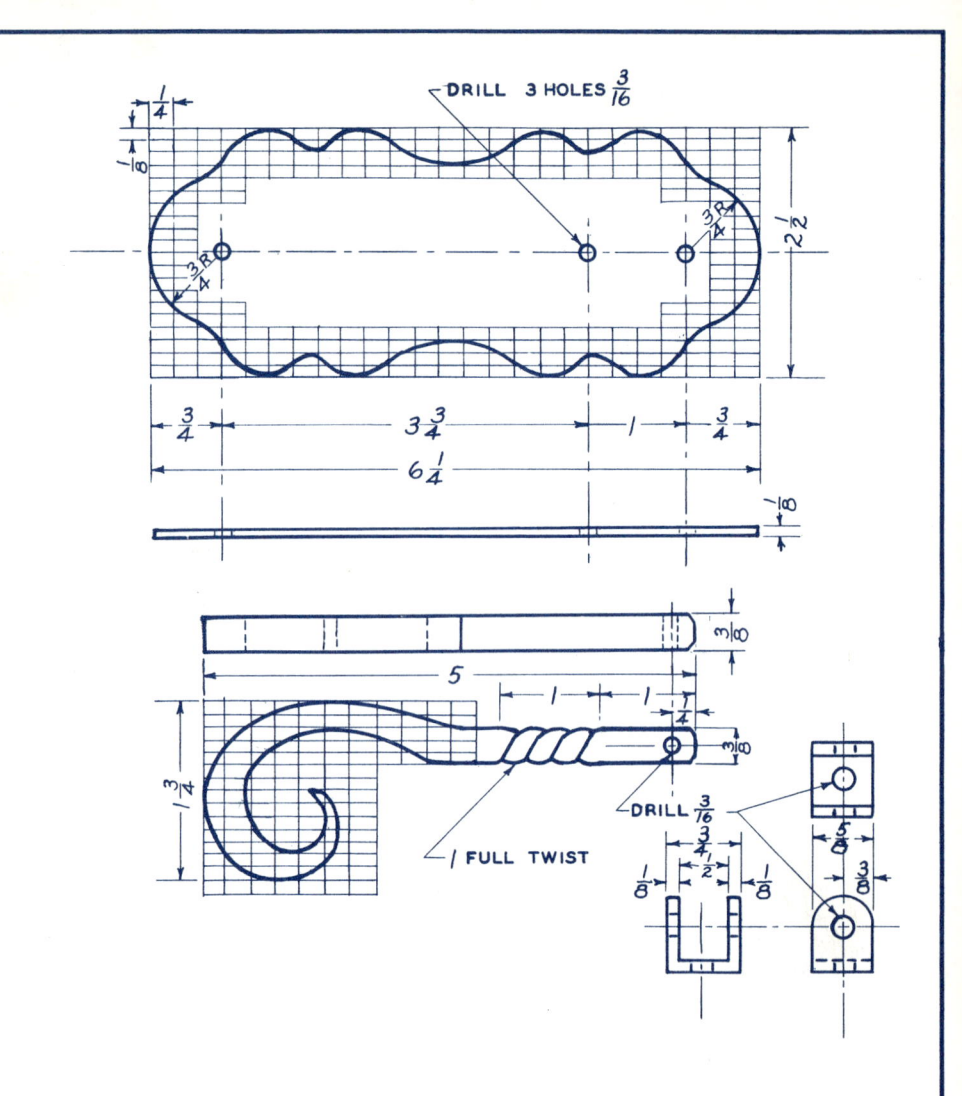

DOOR KNOCKER

Project 20—Door Knocker

This ornamental iron door knocker may be made with many variations. The bracket may be made from a solid piece drilled, filed, and shaped as shown in the print.

Material Required:

1 piece iron, $\frac{1}{8}$ x $2\frac{5}{8}$ x $6\frac{3}{8}$

1 piece iron, $\frac{1}{8}$ x $\frac{5}{8}$ x $2\frac{1}{4}$

1 piece square iron rod, $\frac{3}{8}$ x $6\frac{1}{2}$

1 rivet, S. I., R. H., $\frac{3}{16}$ x $\frac{1}{2}$

1 rivet, S. I., R. H., $\frac{3}{16}$ x 1

References:

Ludwig, *Metalwork Technology and Practice*
Dragoo & Reed, *General Shop Metalwork*
Smith, *Forging and Welding*

Procedure:

1. Design — make pattern.
2. Get out stock.
3. Paste pattern to piece, or mark design with scriber.
4. Work to shape with hacksaw and file.
5. Lay out the holes and center punch.
6. Peen finish.
7. Drill holes as shown, countersink center hole.
8. Get out stock for knocker.
9. Taper end by forging while hot.
10. Shape scroll.
11. Peen finish.
12. Twist one turn as shown.
13. Center punch and drill $\frac{3}{16}$" hole in knocker.
14. Get out stock for bracket.
15. Shape bracket as shown.
16. Lay out, center punch, and drill $\frac{3}{16}$" holes.
17. Assemble bracket to back.
18. Assemble knocker. Do not set hinge too tight.
19. Smooth with file and emery cloth.
20. Blacken entire knocker.
21. Rub with emery cloth.
22. Finish with clear lacquer.

Related Study:

Design
Ornamental finishes

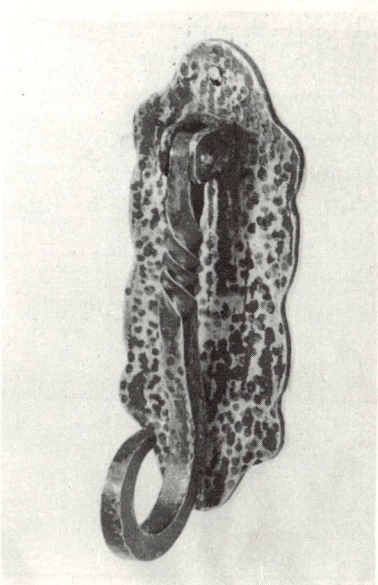

Project 21—Flower Bud Holder

This is especially suitable for rosebuds. A pair of these would be a gift welcomed by any flower lover.

Material Required:
1 piece aluminum, .051 x 3½ dia.
1 piece aluminum, .032 x 1 x 18½
1 test tube, ¾ dia.
1 rivet, aluminum, ⅛ x ½

References:
Ludwig, *Metalwork Technology and Practice*
Dragoo & Reed, *General Shop Metalwork*

Procedure:
1. Get out stock.
2. Cut metal for base (3½" circle).
3. Shape by hammering or pressing.
4. Lay out the scroll.
5. Get out stock for scroll.
6. Drill holes for test tube and rivet.
7. Peen surfaces of base and scroll piece.
8. Form to shape.
9. Rivet scroll to base.
10. Check.
11. Finish with steel wool and polish.

Related Study:
Shaping and forming by hammering
Shaping with the use of jigs

½ INCH SQUARES

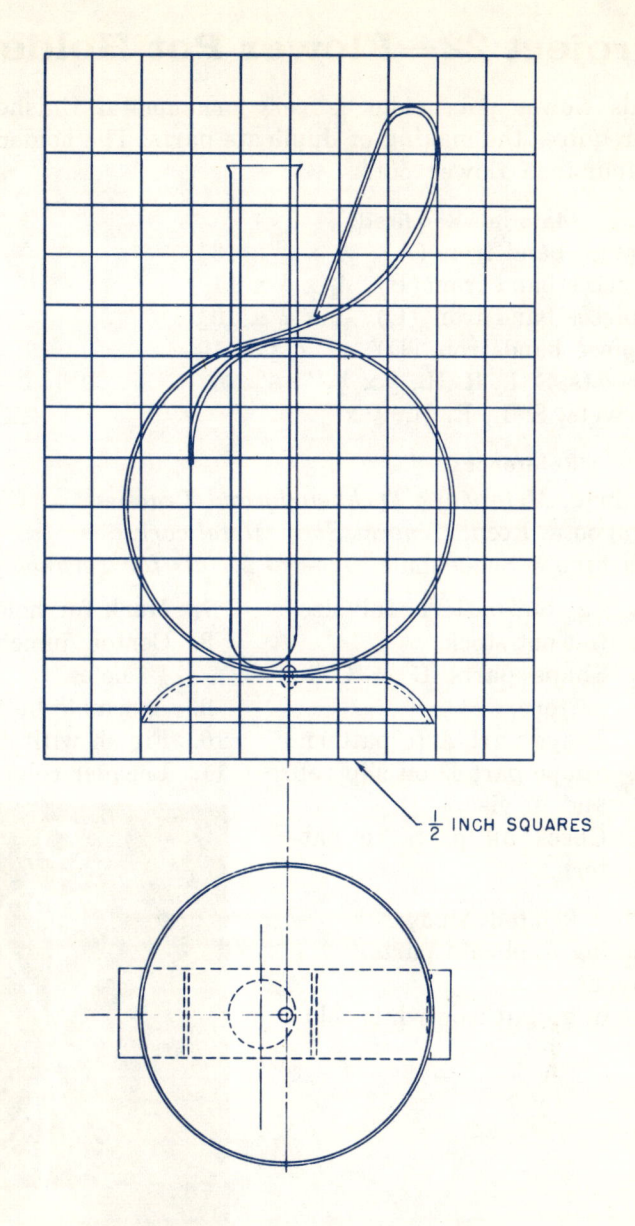

FLOWER BUD HOLDER

Project 22—Flower Pot Holder

This flower pot holder is very ornamental finished in color. It requires the making of duplicate parts. The holder shown fits a four-inch flower pot.

Material Required:
1 piece band iron (A), $\frac{1}{16}$ x $\frac{1}{2}$ x $13\frac{1}{2}$
2 pieces band iron (B), $\frac{1}{16}$ x $\frac{1}{2}$ x 14
2 pieces band iron (C), $\frac{1}{16}$ x $\frac{1}{2}$ x $10\frac{1}{2}$
1 piece band iron (D), $\frac{1}{16}$ x $\frac{1}{2}$ x 15
2 rivets, S. I., R. H., $\frac{1}{8}$ x $\frac{1}{2}$
2 rivets, S. I., R. H., $\frac{1}{8}$ x $\frac{3}{4}$

References:
Ludwig, *Metalwork Technology and Practice*
Dragoo & Reed, *General Shop Metalwork*
Giachino & Schoenhals, *General Metals for Technology*

1. Lay out pattern, full size.
2. Get out stock.
3. Shape parts B & C to pattern.
4. Shape part A to pattern.
5. Shape part D on slip roll and in vise.
6. Check all parts to pattern.
7. Mark for holes.
8. Center punch and drill $\frac{1}{8}''$ holes.
9. Assemble by riveting.
10. Finish with emery cloth.
11. Lacquer color desired.

Related Study:
Making duplicate parts
Layout
Bending light iron while cold

FLOWER POT HOLDER

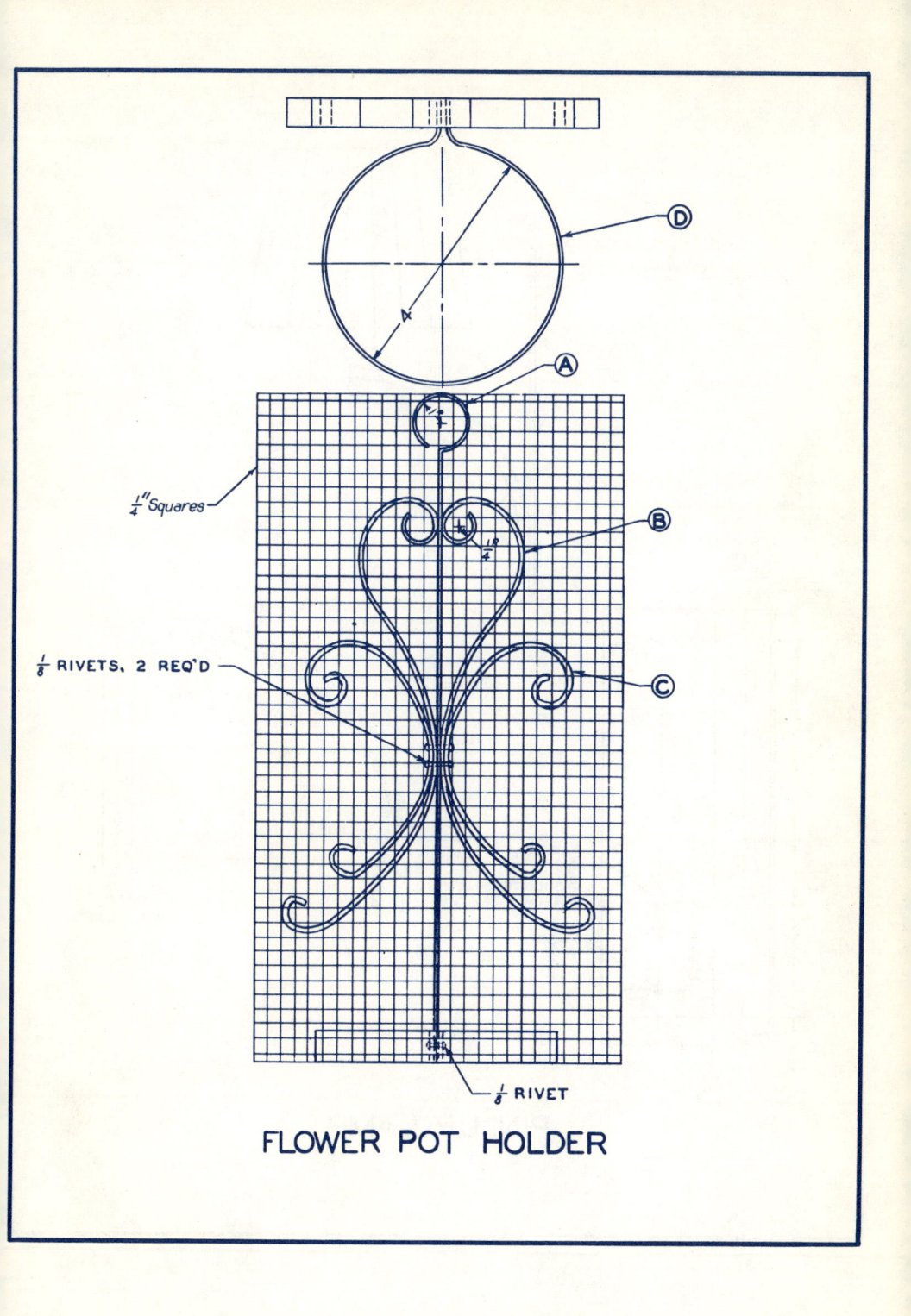

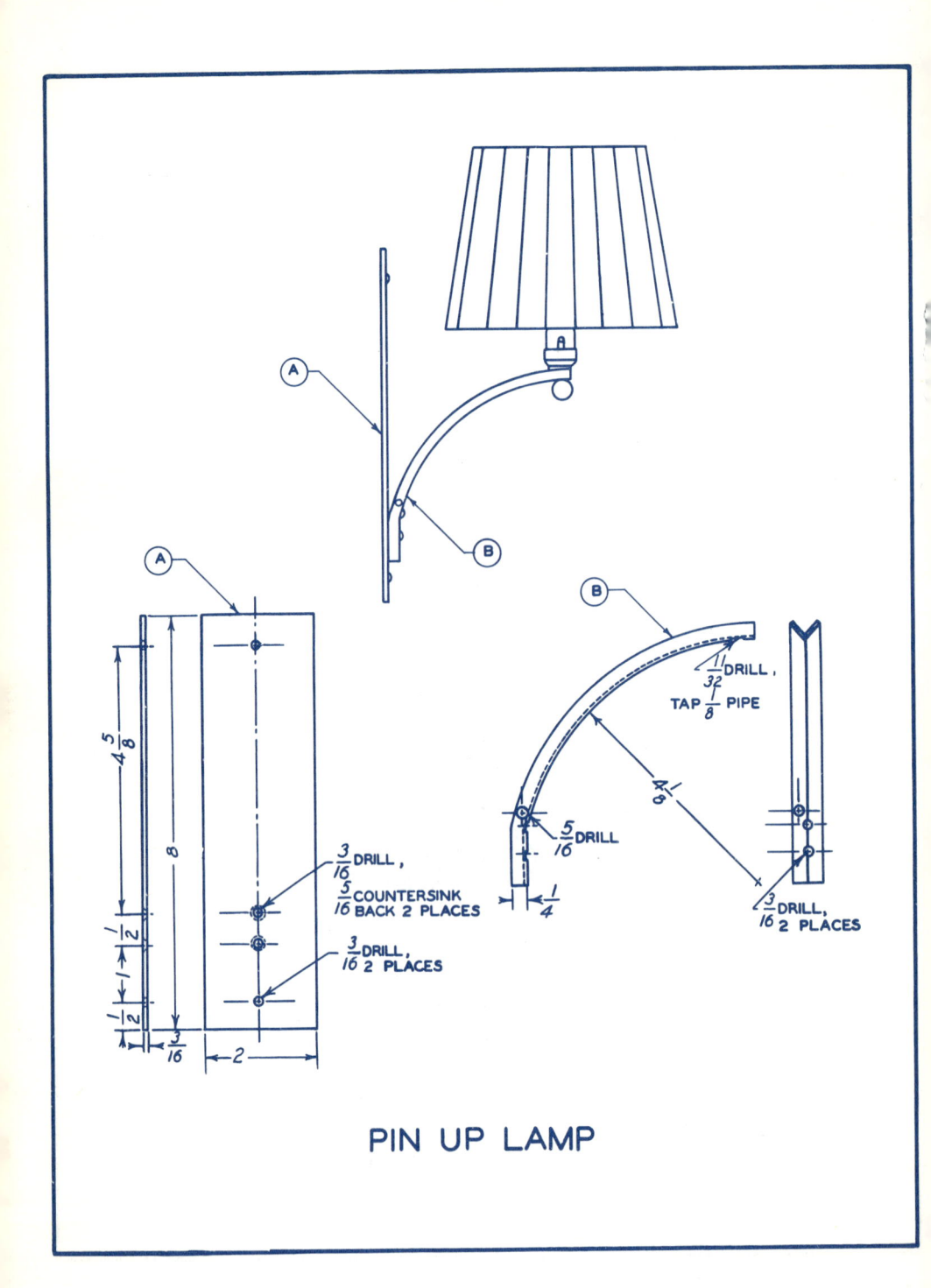

PIN UP LAMP

Project 23—Pin-Up Lamp

A pin-up lamp that may be made with many variations. The materials used may be mild steel or aluminum. The back may be designed or left plain, as desired.

Material Required:
1 piece mild steel, $\frac{3}{16}$ x 2 x 8
2 rivets, S.I., R.H., $\frac{1}{8}$ x $\frac{3}{4}$
1 electric socket
1 piece angle iron, $\frac{1}{8}$ x $\frac{1}{2}$ x $\frac{1}{2}$ x $6\frac{1}{2}$
1 nipple, $\frac{1}{8}$ x $\frac{3}{4}$
1 lamp shade
8 feet lamp cord and plug

References:
Ludwig, *Metalwork Technology and Practice*
Giachino & Schoenhals, *General Metals for Technology*
Dragoo & Reed, *General Shop Metalwork*

Procedure:
Part A.
1. Get out stock.
2. Lay out.
3. Cut off with hack saw.
4. Square one end with file.
5. Lay off length and holes.
6. File to length and shape.
7. Drill holes.
8. Countersink holes.
9. Smooth with file and emery cloth.

Part B.
1. Get out stock.
2. Lay out.
3. Cut to length.
4. Square ends.
5. Lay out the holes.
6. Drill holes as shown.
7. Form as indicated.
8. Tap $\frac{11}{32}$" hole.
9. Smooth with file and emery cloth.
10. Assemble parts A & B.
11. Finish as desired.
12. Wire lamp.

Related Study:
Shaping angle iron
Countersinking
Design
Tapping
Pipe threads

Project 24—Pin-Up Lamp

A very useful project that involves many different operations. The lamp may be used in a den, or as a bed lamp. May be finished with lacquer, or with a peen finish.

Material Required:
1 piece band iron, $\frac{1}{8}$ x $\frac{3}{4}$ x $14\frac{1}{2}$
1 piece band iron, $\frac{1}{8}$ x $\frac{3}{4}$ x $13\frac{1}{2}$
1 piece band iron, $\frac{1}{8}$ x $\frac{3}{4}$ x 8
1 ornament, to be selected
1 piece brass pipe, $\frac{1}{8}$ x 3
3 rivets, soft iron, round heads, $\frac{3}{16}$ x $\frac{1}{2}$
1 each, socket, lamp cord, shade

References:
Ludwig, *Metalwork Technology and Practice*
Smith, *Forging and Welding*
Dragoo & Reed, *General Shop Metalwork*
Smith, *Bench Metalwork*

Procedure:
1. Cut stock to length.
2. Forge ends of scrolls.
3. Dress with file.
4. Shape scrolls to pattern.
5. Lay out the holes.
6. Center punch.
7. Drill holes as shown.
8. Tap $\frac{11}{32}''$ hole.
9. Assemble scrolls with $\frac{3}{16}''$ rivets, heading the rivets.
10. Finish with emery cloth.
11. Finish by lacquering a color or use clear lacquer if surface is peened.
12. Assemble socket, cord.
    NOTE: if ornament is available, finish and assemble it as step No. 10a.

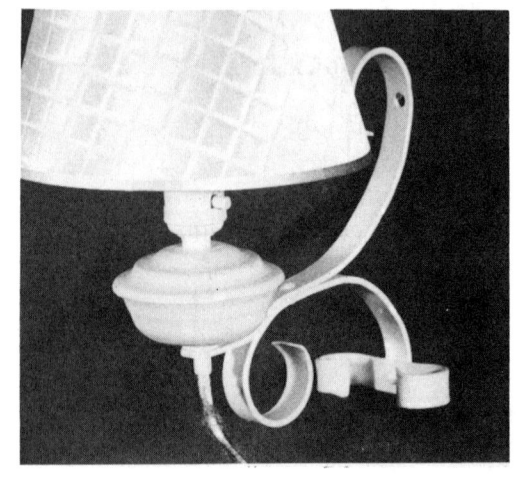

Related Study:
How to shape scrolls, etc.
Pipe threads
Tapping
Wiring lamp

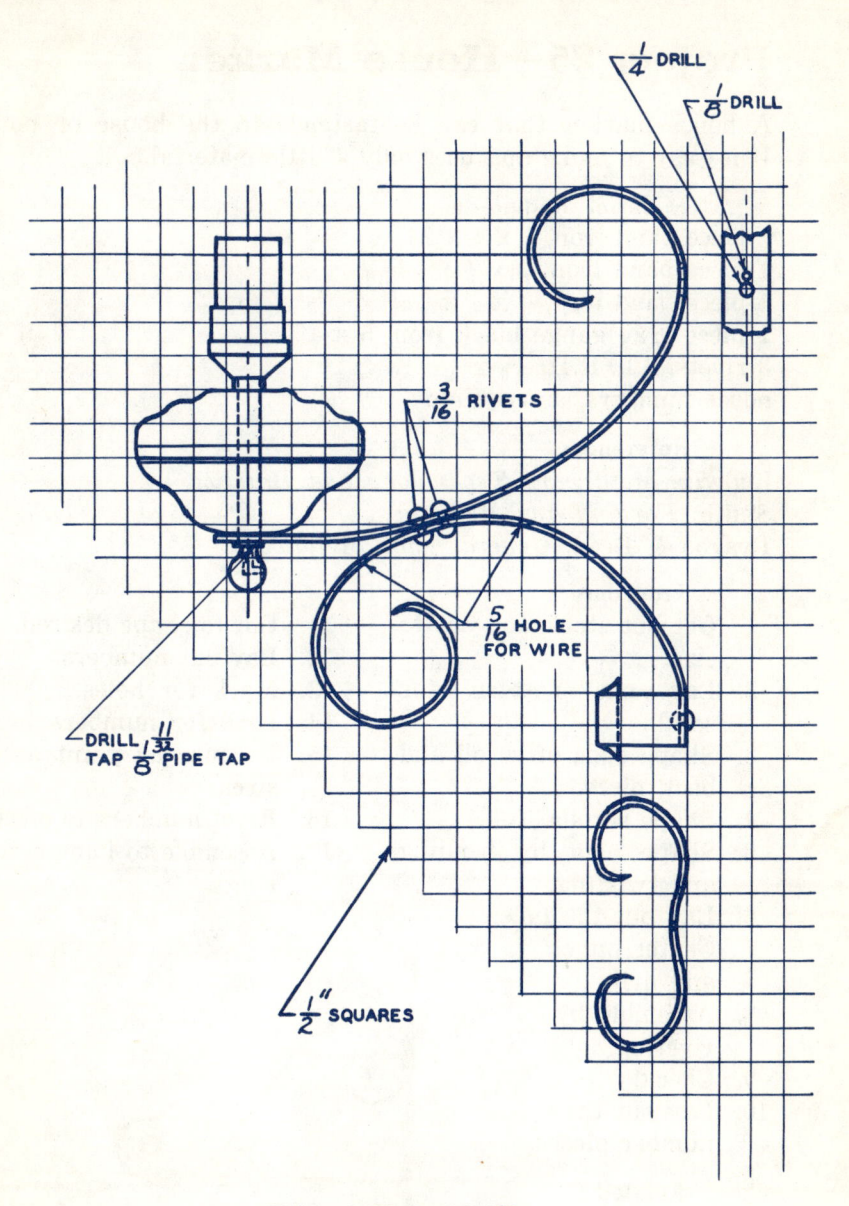

PIN UP LAMP

Project 25 — House Marker

A house marker that can be fastened to the house or porch. It is easy to make and uses only a little material.

Material Required:
1 piece band iron, $\frac{1}{8}$ x $\frac{1}{2}$ x 24
1 piece band iron, $\frac{1}{8}$ x $\frac{1}{2}$ x $14\frac{1}{2}$
1 piece band iron, $\frac{1}{8}$ x 1 x $11\frac{1}{2}$
1 piece #24 gauge black iron, 5 x 15
3 rivets, S.I., R.H., $\frac{3}{16}$ x $\frac{1}{2}$
house numbers, as required

References:
Ludwig, *Metalwork Technology and Practice*
Smith, *Forging and Welding*
Dragoo & Reed, *General Shop Metalwork*

Procedure:
1. Get out stock and cut to size.
2. Lay out pattern for scroll.
3. Shape ends of scroll and back piece.
4. Shape scrolls.
5. Shape arm by bending and twisting.
6. Lay out the holes.
7. Center punch and drill.
8. Assemble by riveting.
9. Check.
10. Lay out the number pieces.
11. Cut to shape desired.
12. Lay out numbers.
13. Mark for holes.
14. Drill for numbers.
15. Lacquer or paint as desired.
16. Rivet numbers to piece.
17. Assemble to hanger with rings.

Related Study:
Layout for scrolls
Twisting metal
Heading rivets

HOUSE MARKER

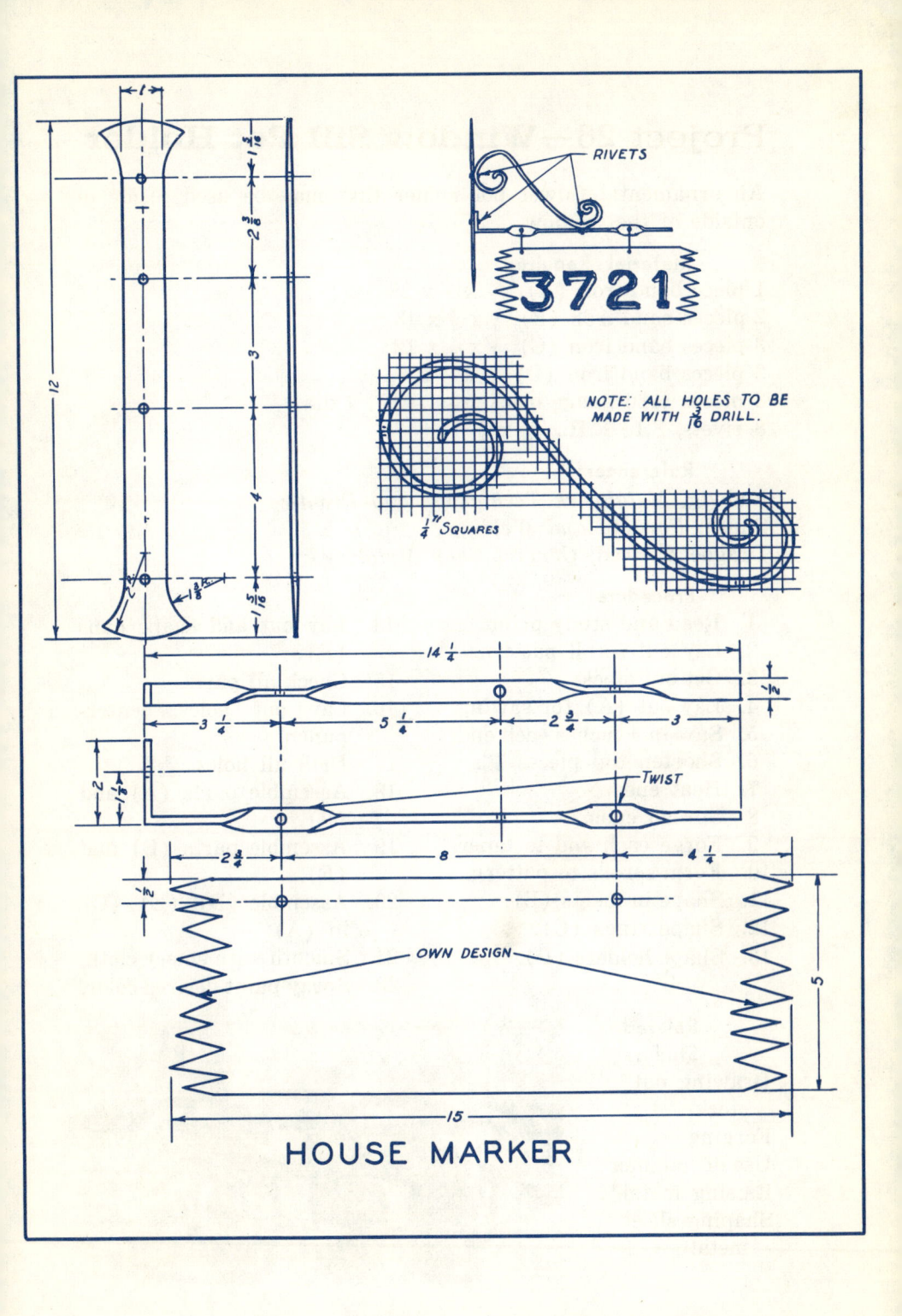

Project 26—Window Sill Pot Holder

An ornamental flower pot holder that may be used inside or outside of the window.

Material Required:
1 piece band iron (A), $\frac{3}{16}$ x 1 x 28
2 pieces band iron (B), $\frac{1}{8}$ x $\frac{1}{2}$ x 13
3 pieces band iron (C), $\frac{1}{8}$ x $\frac{1}{2}$ x 12
3 pieces band iron (D), $\frac{1}{8}$ x $\frac{1}{2}$ x $6\frac{1}{2}$
3 pieces #26 gauge black iron, (E), 4 dia.
8 rivets, S.I., R.H., $\frac{3}{16}$ x $\frac{1}{2}$

References:
Ludwig, *Metalwork Technology and Practice*
Smith, *Forging and Welding*
Dragoo & Reed, *General Shop Metalwork*

Procedure:
1. Read and study print.
2. Lay out scroll patterns.
3. Get out stock.
4. Lay out (A) for sawing.
5. Saw in 4 inches each end.
6. Shorten top pieces 1".
7. Heat ends.
8. Spread ends.
9. Forge each end to taper.
10. Form scrolls to pattern.
11. Shape brackets (B).
12. Shape rings (C).
13. Shape holders (D).
14. Lay out and shape pans (E).
15. Check all parts.
16. Lay out holes, center-punch.
17. Drill all holes, $\frac{3}{16}$".
18. Assemble parts (A) and (B).
19. Assemble parts (D) and (E).
20. Assemble (D), (E), (C) to (A).
21. Smooth with emery cloth.
22. Spray paint desired color.

Related Study:
Drawing out stock
Forging
Use of hammer
Raising metal
Shaping sheet metal

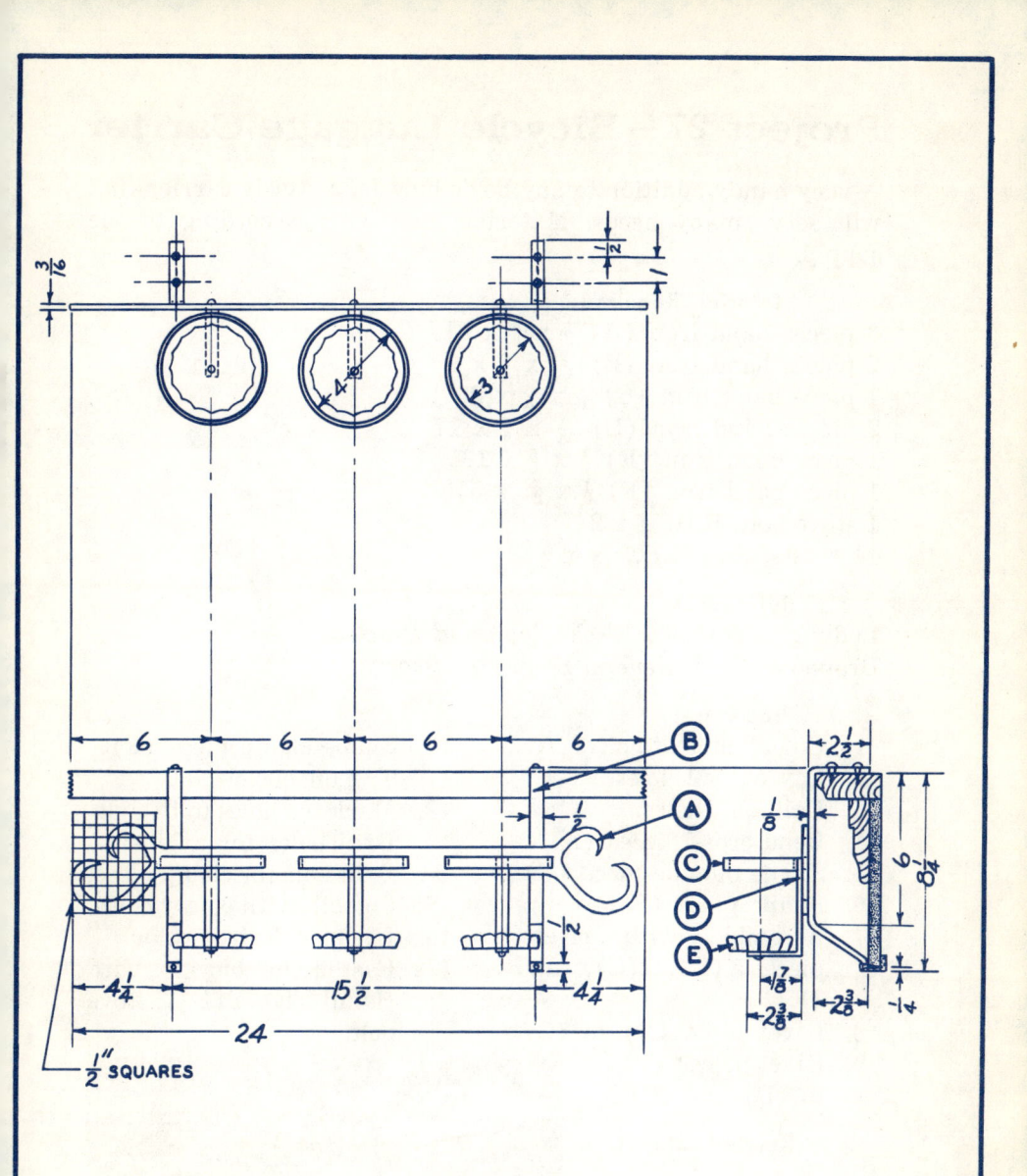

WINDOW SILL POT HOLDER

Project 27—Bicycle Luggage Carrier

A very handy addition to any boy's bicycle, a sturdy carrier that will serve many needs. Materials may vary according to the supply.

Material Required:
3 pieces band iron (A) $\frac{1}{8}$ x $\frac{5}{8}$ x $8\frac{1}{4}$
2 pieces band iron (B) $\frac{3}{16}$ x $\frac{5}{8}$ x 9
1 piece band iron (C) $\frac{1}{8}$ x $\frac{5}{8}$ x 29
2 pieces band iron (D) $\frac{3}{16}$ x $\frac{5}{8}$ x 17
1 piece band iron (E) $\frac{1}{8}$ x $\frac{5}{8}$ x $18\frac{1}{2}$
1 piece band iron (F) $\frac{1}{8}$ x $\frac{5}{8}$ x $5\frac{1}{2}$
1 stove bolt, R.H., $\frac{1}{4}$ x 2
14 rivets, S.I., R.H., $\frac{3}{16}$ x $\frac{1}{2}$

References:
Ludwig, *Metalwork Technology and Practice*
Dragoo & Reed, *General Shop Metalwork*

Procedure:
1. Cut all stock to size.
2. Lay out all holes.
3. Drill $\frac{3}{16}$" holes.
4. Bend cross pieces (A).
5. Shape outside piece (C).
6. Shape piece (E).
7. Assemble with rivets, pieces (A), (C), and (E).
8. Rivet piece (D) to (C).
9. Rivet pieces (B) to (D) and (C).
10. Shape clamp piece (F).
11. Try on bicycle.
12. Mark for holes to fit axle.
13. Drill holes for axle.
14. Drill hole for clamp piece.
15. Smooth with emery cloth.
16. Lacquer desired color.
17. Fasten to bicycle with clamp (F) and $\frac{1}{4}$" stove bolt.

Related Study:
Riveting
Lacquer
Spray painting
Laying out duplicate pieces

LUGGAGE CARRIER

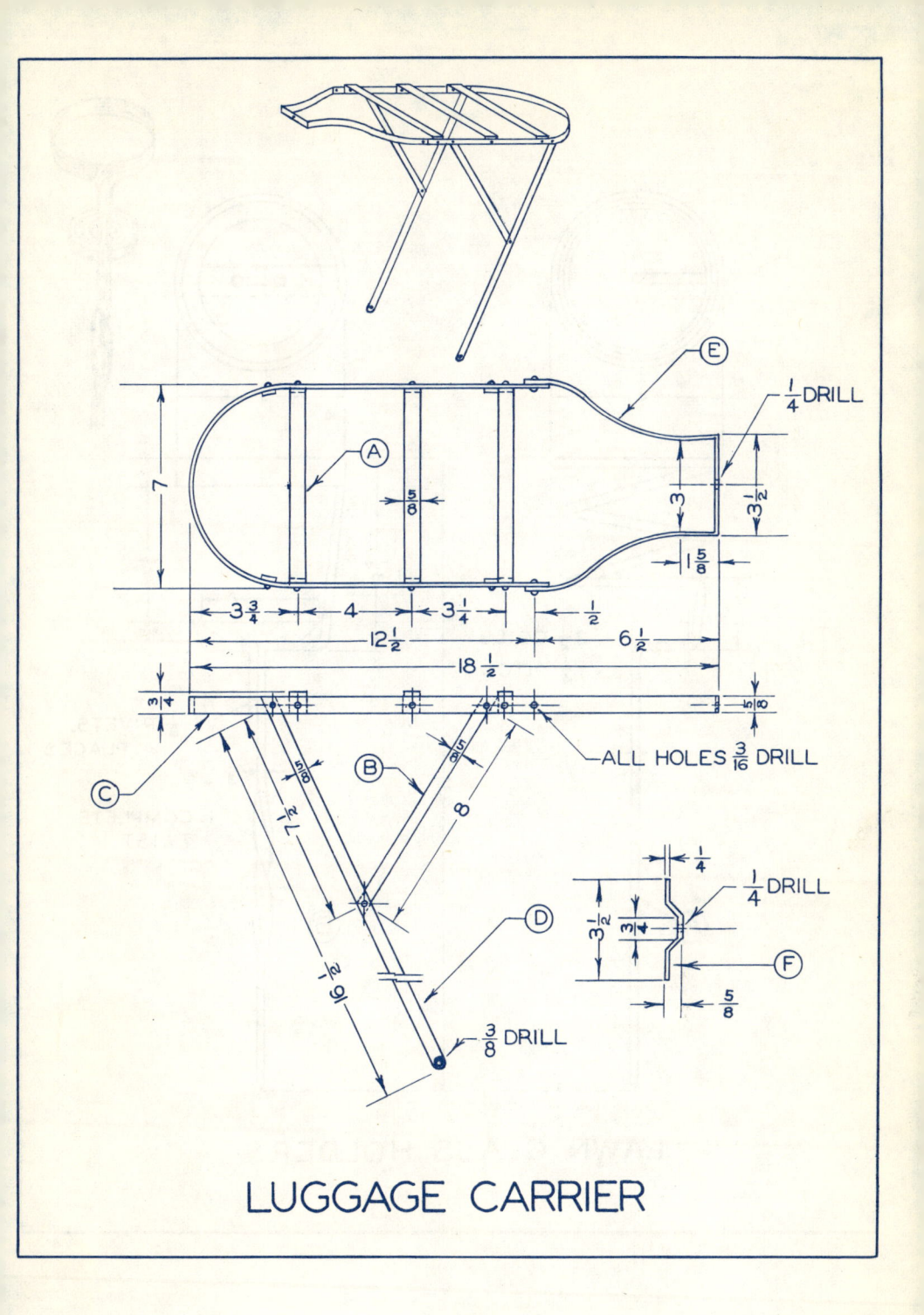

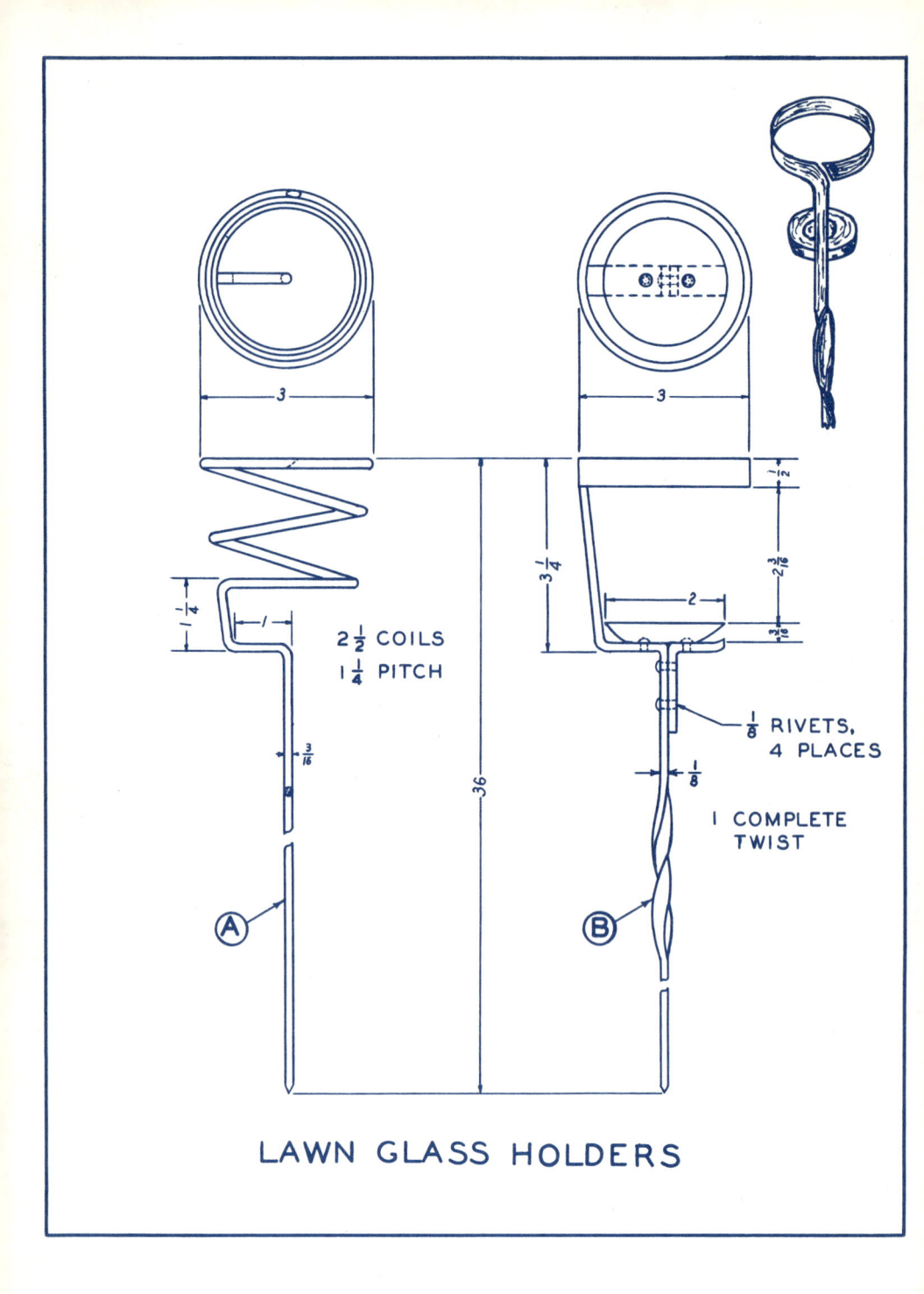

LAWN GLASS HOLDERS

Project 28—Lawn Glass Holder

These holders will be very useful by your lawn chairs to hold glasses or soft drink bottles. Make a number of them.

Material Required:
Holder (A): 1 piece round iron rod, $\frac{3}{16}$ or $\frac{1}{4}$ x 65
Holder (B): 1 piece band iron, $\frac{1}{8}$ x $\frac{1}{2}$ x 52
         1 piece band iron, $\frac{1}{8}$ x $\frac{1}{2}$ x $2\frac{1}{4}$
         1 piece #22 gauge black iron, 2 dia.
         2 rivets, soft iron, round heads, $\frac{1}{8}$ x $\frac{3}{8}$

References:
Ludwig, *Metalwork Technology and Practice*
Smith, *Forging and Welding*
Dragoo & Reed, *General Shop Metalwork*

Procedure:

Holder B
1. Get out stock.
2. Shape top to 3" dia.
3. Heat and bend at right angles.
4. Lay out the bends.
5. Bend to shape.
6. Lay out the bracket.
7. Bend to shape.
8. Lay out the holes.
9. Drill $\frac{1}{8}$" holes.
10. Assemble bracket to upright.
11. Rivet bracket to upright.
12. Rivet bottom to bracket.
13. Twist upright one turn.
14. Sharpen end.
15. Check holder.
16. Finish with emery cloth.
17. Lacquer desired color.

Holder A
1. Cut stock to length.
2. Flatten coil end; smooth.
3. Start scroll over 3" pipe.
4. Clamp scroll to pipe.
5. Make $2\frac{1}{2}$ coils.
6. Remove from pipe.
7. Stretch out coils to shape.
8. Lay out the bends.
9. Bend to shape.
10. Sharpen end.
11. Check holder.
12. Finish with emery cloth.
13. Lacquer desired color.

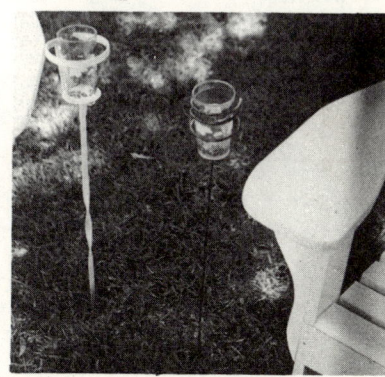

Related Study:
Shaping coils
Forming metal while hot
Twisting metal

Project 29—Door Grill

A grill that will not only add beauty to your home, but will protect the screen wire.

Material Required:
2 pieces band iron, $\frac{1}{8}$ x $\frac{3}{8}$ x 51
4 pieces band iron, $\frac{1}{8}$ x $\frac{3}{8}$ x 32
9 rivets, S.I., R.H., $\frac{1}{8}$ x $\frac{1}{2}$

References:
Ludwig, *Metalwork Technology and Practice*
Dragoo & Reed, *General Shop Metalwork*

Procedure:
1. Get out stock and cut to size.
2. Shape scrolls on each end.
3. Lay out and mark the twists.
4. Twist as shown or desired.
5. Lay out the holes and center punch.
6. Drill the $\frac{1}{8}''$ holes for riveting.
7. Assemble and check.
8. Rivet, head both sides of rivet.
9. Check on door.
10. Mark for holes used in fastening.
11. Drill $\frac{3}{16}''$ holes for wood screws.
12. Smooth with emery cloth.
13. Finish desired color.

Related Study:
Twisting metal
Making scrolls
Laying out for twisting
Spray painting
Lacquers

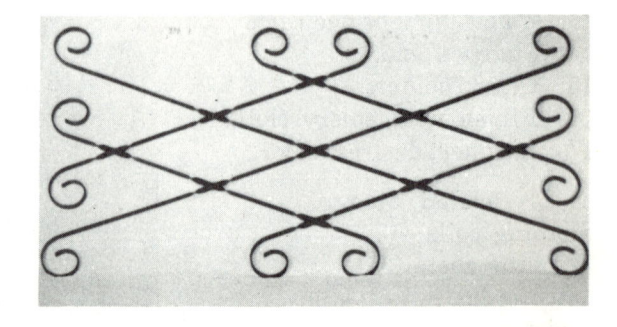

DOOR GRILL

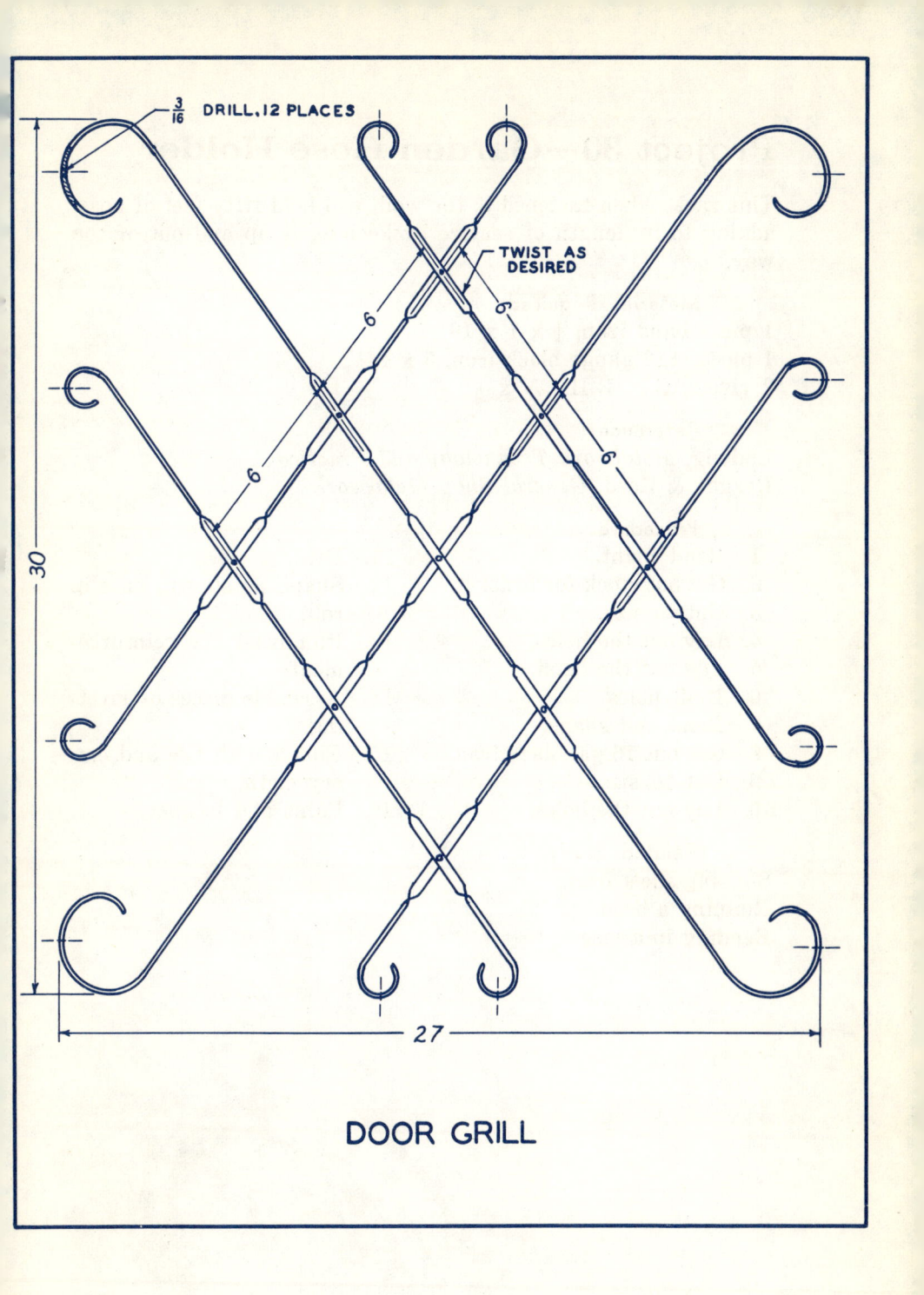

Project 30—Garden Hose Holder

This rack, when fastened to the wall, will hold fifty feet of hose, adding to its length of service by keeping it up and out of the way.

Material Required:
1 piece band iron, $\frac{1}{4}$ x 1 x 18
1 piece #16 gauge black iron, 5 x $14\frac{1}{2}$
2 rivets, S.I., R.H., $\frac{3}{16}$ x $\frac{1}{2}$

References:
Ludwig, *Metalwork Technology and Practice*
Dragoo & Reed, *General Shop Metalwork*

Procedure:
1. Read print.
2. Get out stock for bracket.
3. Cut to size.
4. Lay out the holes.
5. Lay out the bend.
6. Drill holes.
7. Bend and shape.
8. Get out 16 ga. black iron.
9. Cut to size.
10. Lay out the holes.
11. Drill.
12. Shape as shown, on slip roll.
13. Run bead for reinforcement.
14. Assemble pieces by riveting.
15. Finish with file and emery cloth.
16. Paint and lacquer.

Related Study:
Shaping sheet iron
Running a bead
Bending in a vise

GARDEN HOSE HOLDER

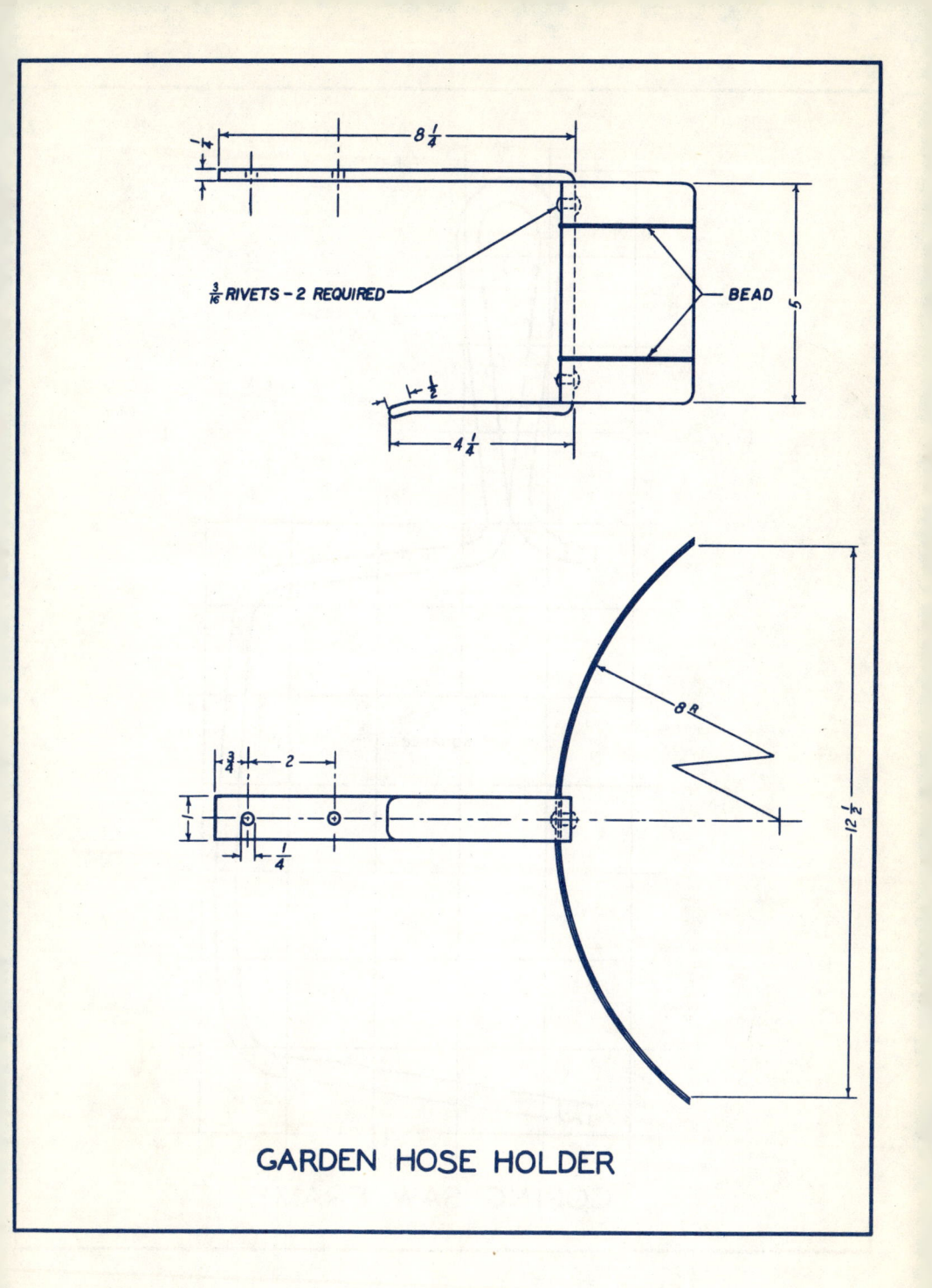

¼" RD. IRON

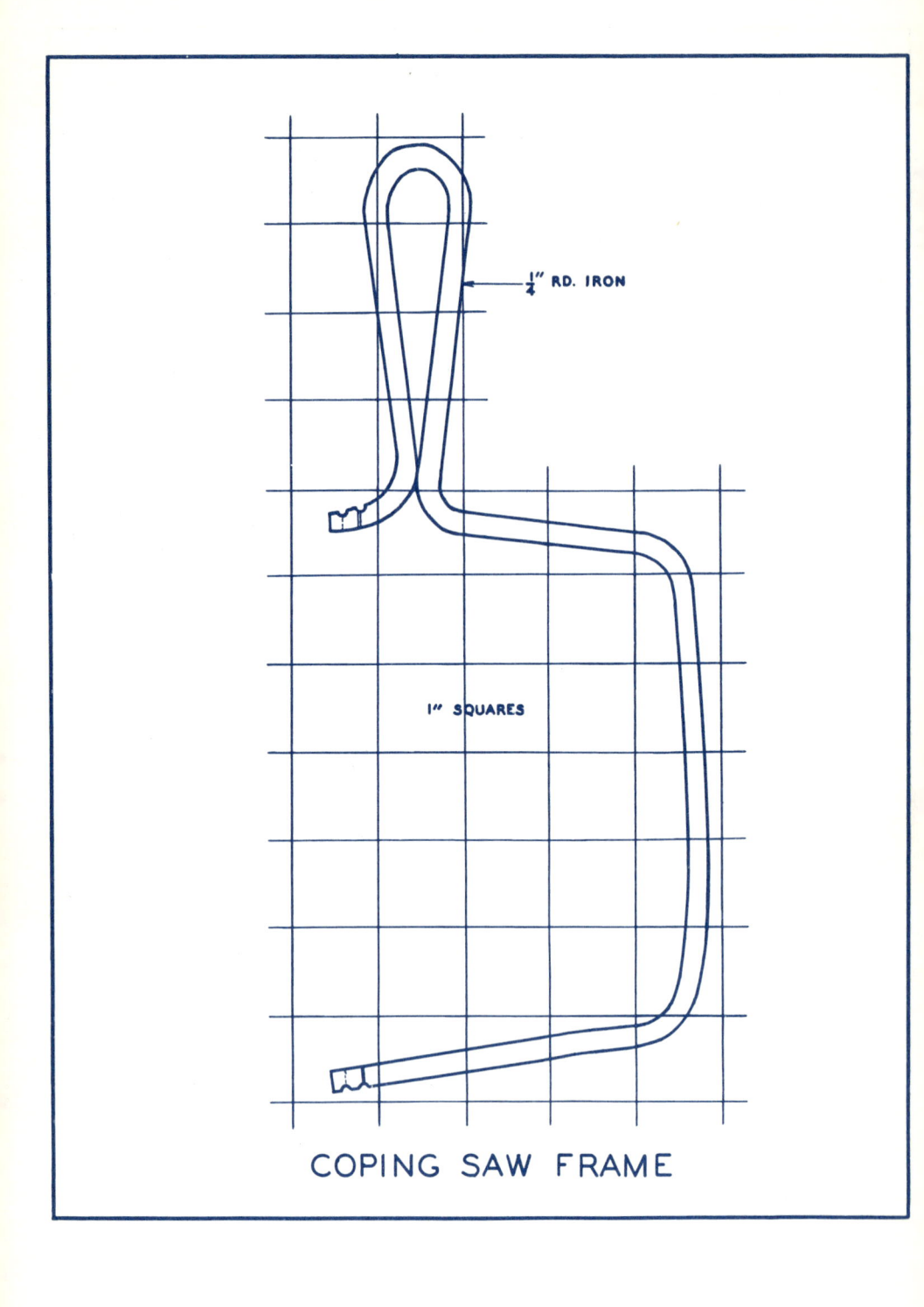

1" SQUARES

COPING SAW FRAME

Project 31—Coping Saw Frame

A piece of equipment that is easily made and is handy around the home workshop. It may be shaped while hot or cold. A cheese cutter may be made by using fine steel wire instead of a saw blade.

Material Required:
1 piece round iron or drill rod, $\frac{1}{4}$ x 22
1 blade, $6\frac{1}{2}$ pin end

References:
Ludwig, *Metalwork Technology and Practice*
Dragoo & Reed, *General Shop Metalwork*
Smith, *Forging and Welding*

Procedure:
1. Lay out pattern.
2. Get out stock and cut to length.
3. Mark with punch for bends.
4. Heat and bend to shape — might use jig with pins to form.
5. Lay out the slots for the blade.
6. Saw slots.
7. Countersink as shown for loop or pin end blades.
8. Finish with a file and emery cloth.

Related Study:
Heating and bending
Proper heat for bending
Laying out patterns
Marking for bending

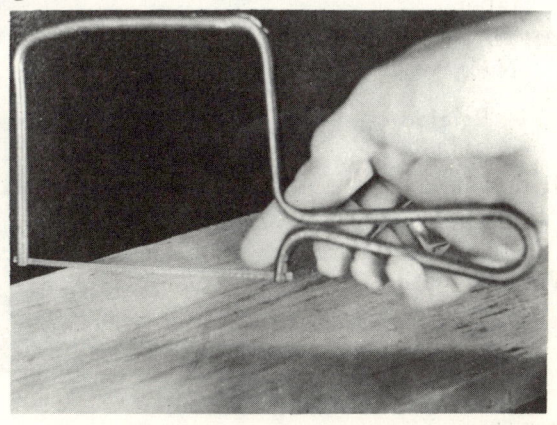

Project 32—Soldering Copper

This is a small soldering copper which anyone can easily make. It is durable and very useful for soldering small work.

Material Required:
1 piece copper, $\frac{3}{4}$ x $\frac{3}{4}$ x $1\frac{1}{2}$
1 piece iron rod, $\frac{5}{16}$ x 10
1 piece round hardwood, 1 x $4\frac{1}{2}$
1 piece ferrule, $\frac{3}{4}$ x $\frac{1}{2}$

References:
Ludwig, *Metalwork Technology and Practice*
Dragoo & Reed, *General Shop Metalwork*
Boyd, *Metalworking*

Procedure:

Point
1. Cut stock to size.
2. Carefully heat copper and forge point.
3. File point and sides smooth.
4. File end.
5. Spot the center.
6. Drill $\frac{9}{32}$" hole for tapping.
7. Tap with $\frac{5}{16}$" N.C.

Shank
1. Get out stock.
2. Forge tang to 1" square taper.
3. Thread other end $\frac{5}{16}$" N.C.

Handle
1. Procure suitable wood.
2. Center and turn as shown.
3. Drill $\frac{1}{4}$" pilot hole.
4. Cut ferrule from $\frac{3}{4}$" pipe.
5. Dress with file and emery cloth.
6. Place on handle.

Assembly
1. Fit shank to copper point.
2. Place the handle on the shank.
3. Check.

Related Study:
Drilling and tapping soft metal
Working with copper

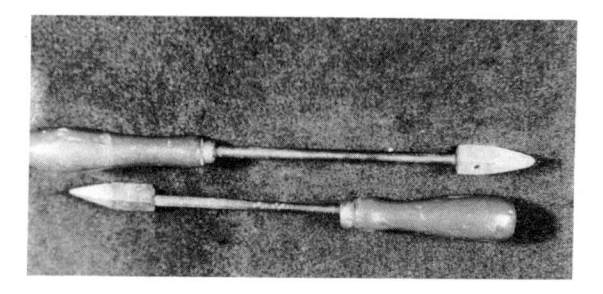

SOLDERING COPPER

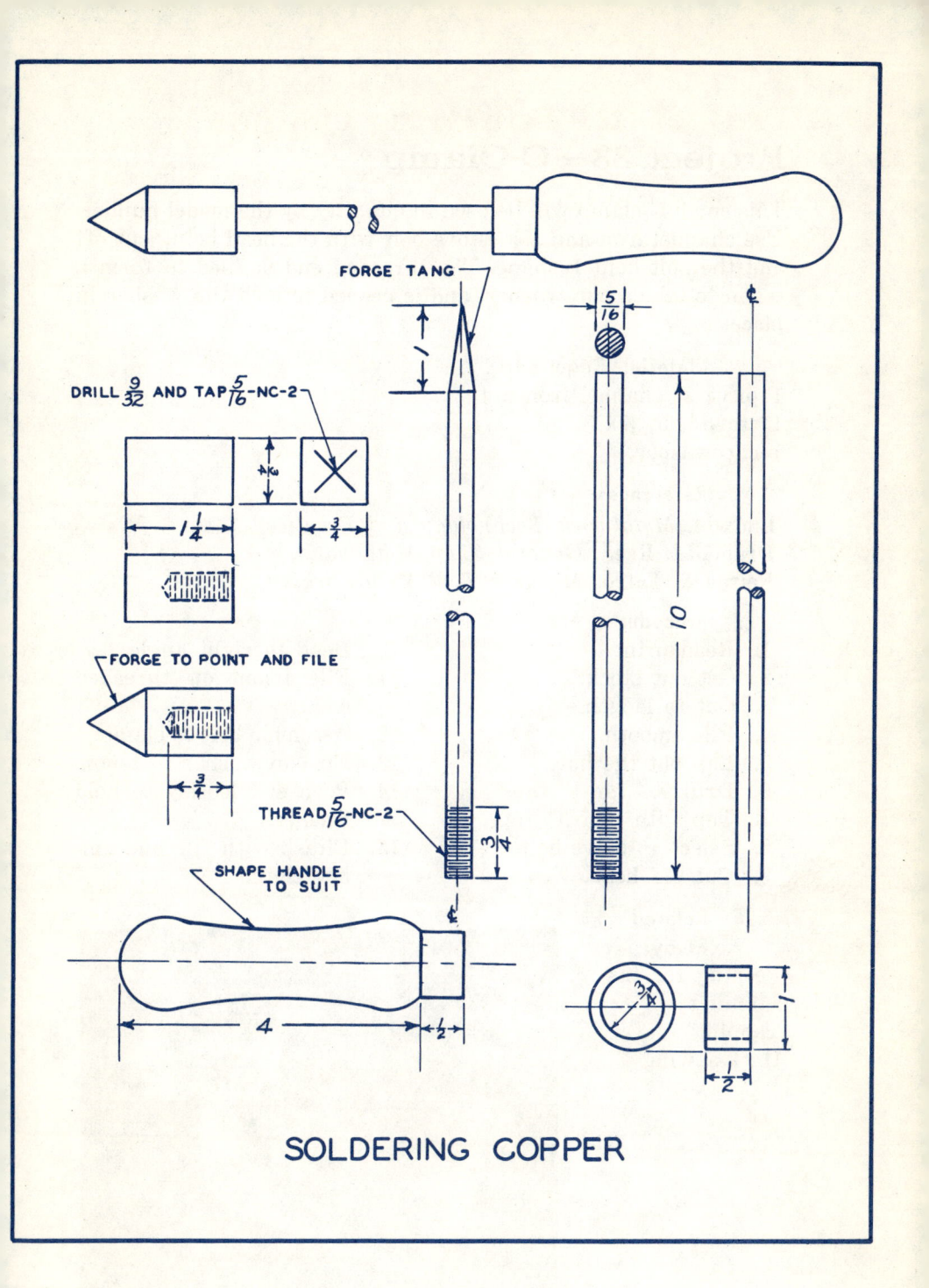

Project 33—C-Clamp

This small C-clamp will be used in quantity by the model builder. Use channel iron and a ¼" stove bolt with the head being cut off and the bolt bent L-shape. The threaded end is filed to form a tenon to take a cup washer, and is peened to hold the washer in place.

Material Required:
1 piece 2" channel iron x 1
1 stove bolt, ¼ x 3
1 cup washer, $\frac{3}{16}$

References:
Ludwig, *Metalwork Technology and Practice*
Dragoo & Reed, *General Shop Metalwork*
Feirer & Tatro, *Machine Tool Metalworking*

Procedure:
1. Read print.
2. Get out stock.
3. Cut to length.
4. File smooth.
5. Lay out the hole.
6. Drill $\frac{7}{32}$" for ¼" tap.
7. Tap with ¼" N.C. tap.
8. Select ¼" stove bolt.
9. Cut off head.
10. Bend to right angle.
11. File tenon on threaded end.
12. Assemble bolt to clamp.
13. Fit cup washer to tenon.
14. Peen end loosely to hold washer.
15. Finish with file and emery cloth.

Related Study:
Peening for fastening
Tapping
Hack-sawing

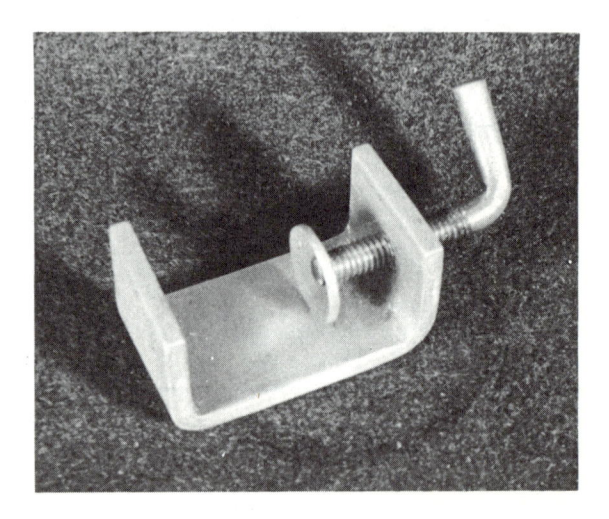

¼ STOVE BOLT

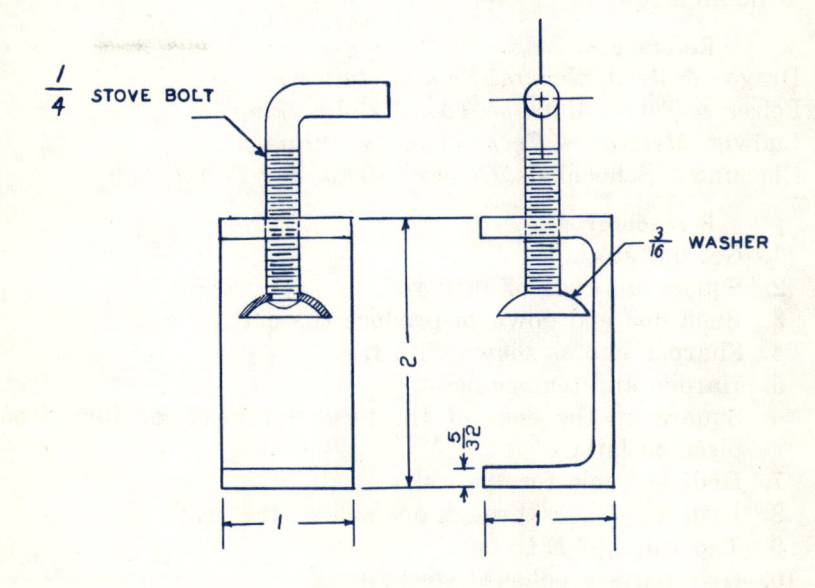

3/16 WASHER

2

5/32

1

1

C-CLAMP

Project 34—Marking Gauge

A project that may be made with or without the use of an engine lathe to turn the head part of the gauge. It is a very useful tool in the home workshop.

Material Required:
1 piece drill rod, $\frac{3}{16}$ x $6\frac{1}{8}$
1 piece steel rod, $\frac{7}{8}$ dia. x $\frac{5}{8}$
1 thumb screw, $\frac{3}{16}$

References:
Dragoo & Reed, *General Shop Metalwork*
Feirer & Tatro, *Machine Tool Metalworking*
Ludwig, *Metalwork Technology and Practice*
Giachino & Schoenhals, *General Metals for Technology*

Procedure:
1. Get out stock.
2. Square up ends of drill rod.
3. Bend one end down to produce the cutting edge.
4. Sharpen end as shown with file.
5. Harden and temper point.
6. Square up the ends of the piece for head, or turn from piece on lathe.
7. Drill $\frac{13}{64}''$ hole for the rod.
8. Drill a $\frac{9}{64}''$ hole through one side of the head.
9. Tap with $\frac{3}{16}''$ N.C. tap.
10. Give parts a polished steel finish.
11. Assemble.

Related Study:
Types of taps
Kinds of threads

MARKING GAUGE

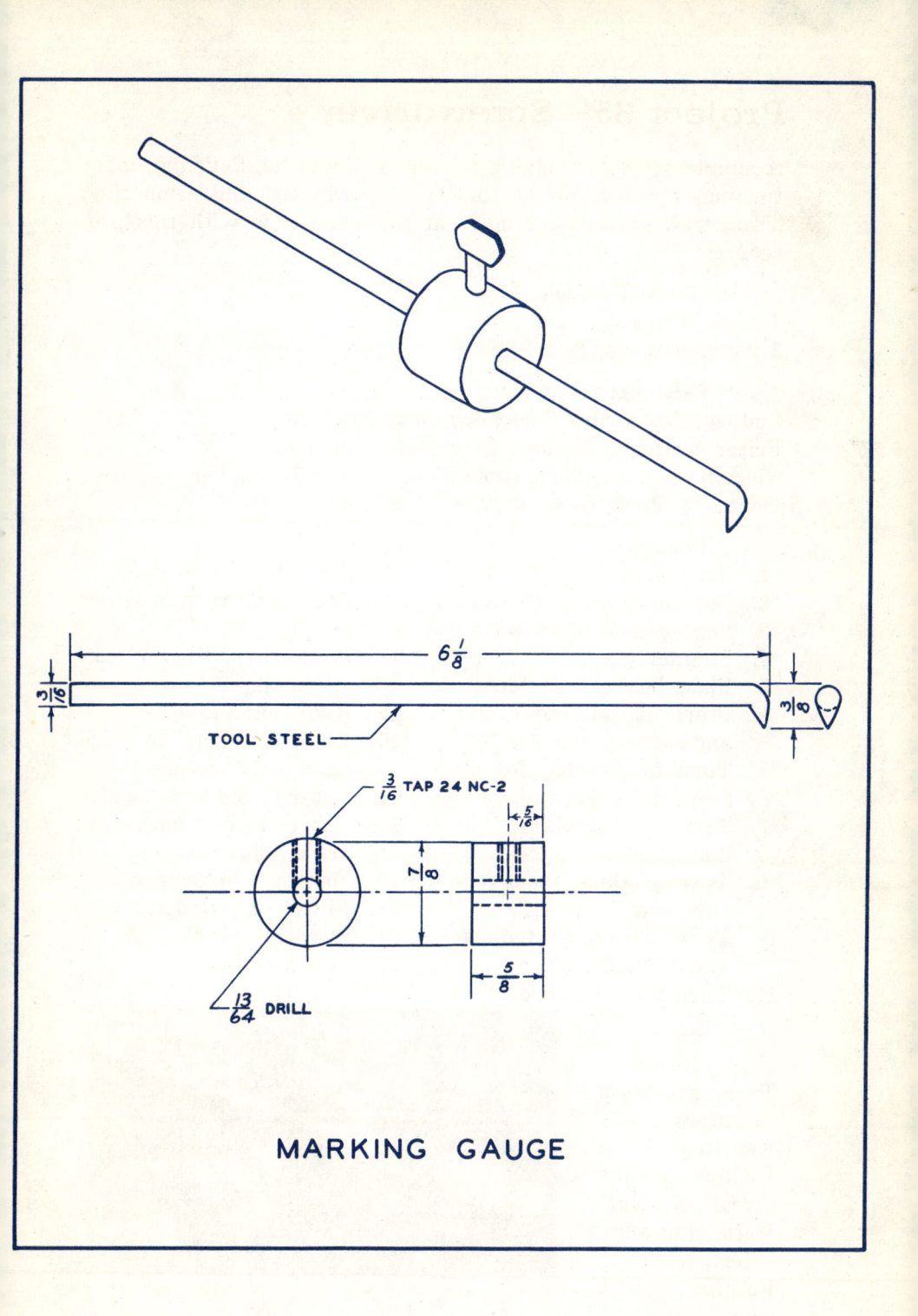

Project 35—Screwdriver

A simple project involving the use of the lathe, knurling, taper turning, drilling, sweat soldering, hardening and tempering. Two screw drivers are made at the same time with this procedure.

Material Required:
1 piece M.S. rod, $\frac{5}{8}$ x 6
1 piece drill rod, $\frac{3}{16}$ x $8\frac{1}{4}$

References:
Ludwig, *Metalwork Technology and Practice*
Feirer & Tatro, *Machine Tool Metalworking*
Giachino & Schoenhals, *General Metals for Technology*
Dragoo & Reed, *General Shop Metalwork*

Procedure:
1. Read print
2. Cut out stock.
3. Center ends of $\frac{5}{8}''$ rod.
4. Countersink.
5. Place between centers.
6. Start at tail stock end and cut to $\frac{1}{2}''$ dia. for $1\frac{1}{2}''$.
7. Turn to $\frac{7}{16}''$ dia. for $\frac{5}{8}''$ from tail stock end.
8. Turn $\frac{1}{8}''$ ferrule $\frac{7}{16}''$ in diameter.
9. Turn $\frac{1}{2}''$ taper from ferrule, end $\frac{5}{16}''$ to $\frac{7}{16}''$.
10. Turn concave $\frac{3}{8}''$ dia. low and $\frac{3}{8}''$ wide.
11. Turn the other end.
12. Cut into two pieces.
13. Check and turn ends per print.
14. Finish with file and emery cloth.
15. Knurl handle.
16. Drill $\frac{3}{16}''$ hole in each handle, 1" deep.
17. Cut drill rod to 4" length.
18. Forge one end for screwdriver bit.
19. Harden and temper.
20. Finish on grinder.
21. Sweat in handle.
22. Polish or blue.

Related Study:
Turning between centers
Knurling
Drilling in lathe
Sweat soldering
Hardening and tempering
Forging

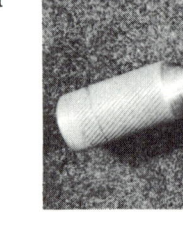

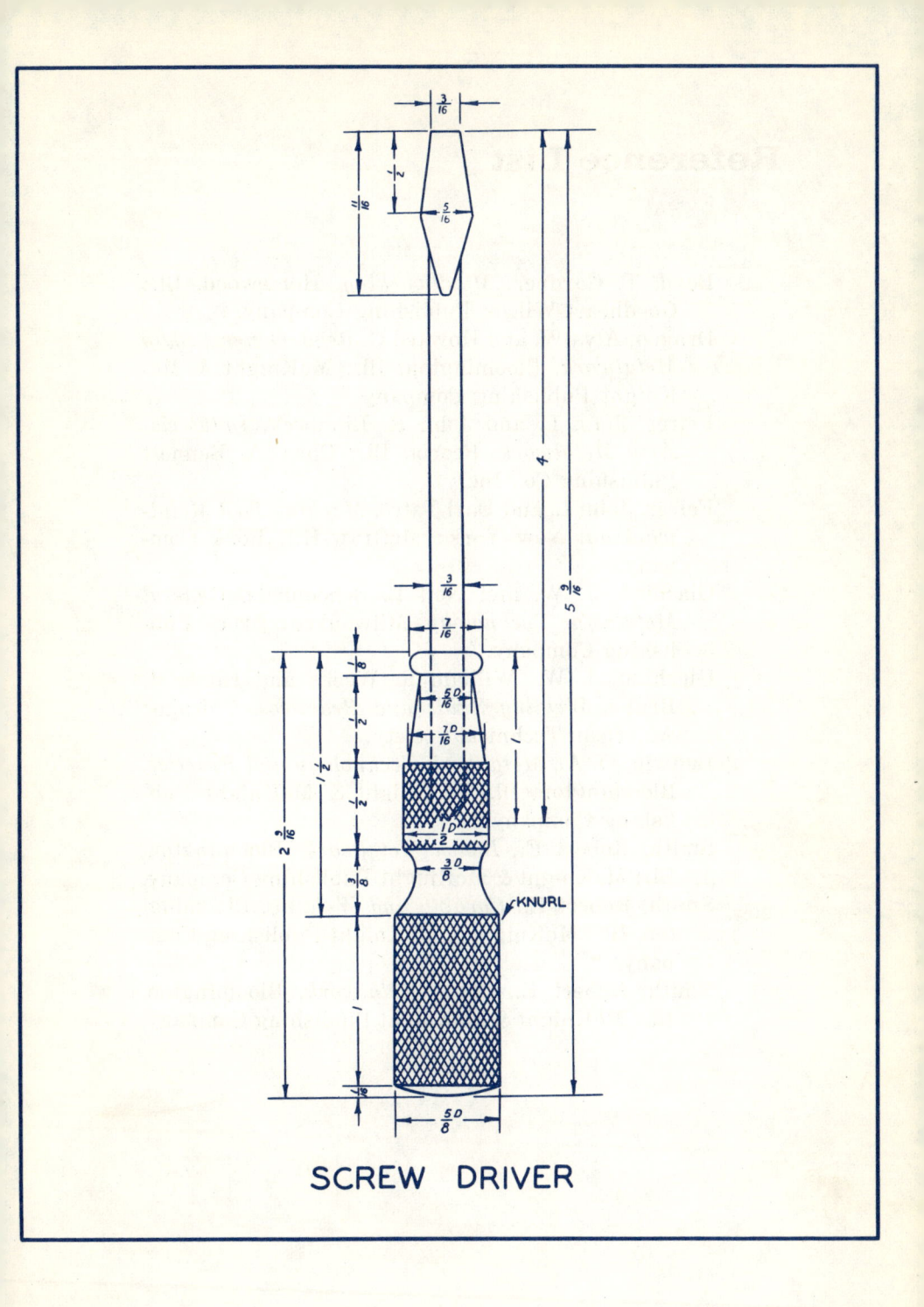

SCREW DRIVER

Reference List

Boyd, T. Gardner, *Metalworking*. Homewood, Ill.: Goodheart-Wilcox Publishing Company.

Dragoo, Alva W. and Howard O. Reed, *General Shop Metalwork*. Bloomington, Ill.: McKnight & McKnight Publishing Company.

Feirer, John L. and John R. Lindbeck, *Industrial Arts Metalwork*. Peoria, Ill.: Chas. A. Bennett Publishing Co., Inc.

Feirer, John L. and Earl Tatro, *Machine Tool Metalworking*. New York: McGraw-Hill Book Company.

Giachino, J. W. and Neil L. Schoenhals, *General Metals for Technology*. Milwaukee: Bruce Publishing Company.

Giachino, J. W., William R. Weeks and Elmer J. Brune, *Welding Skills and Practices*. Chicago: American Technical Society.

Ludwig, O. A., *Metalwork Technology and Practice*. Bloomington, Ill.: McKnight & McKnight Publishing Company.

Smith, Robert E., *Bench Metalwork*. Bloomington, Ill.: McKnight & McKnight Publishing Company.

Smith, Robert E., *Forging and Welding*. Bloomington, Ill.: McKnight & McKnight Publishing Company.

Smith, Robert E., *Sheet Metalwork*. Bloomington, Ill.: McKnight & McKnight Publishing Company.